POVERTY MINDSET VS ABUNDANCE MINDSET

Sunday Adelaja

Sunday Adelaja
Poverty Mindset Vs Abundance Mindset
©2017 Sunday Adelaja
ISBN 978-1-908040-32-9

Cover design by Alexander Bondaruk
Interior design by Olena Kotelnykova

CONTENTS

INTRODUCTION

No one likes to live in poverty. No one wants to be poor. Everyone will love to live in abundance and so many people strive for this, but very few people get to achieve this status of living in abundance. As sad as this may seem, this is the reality in our world today. Over 50% of our world population today lives in lack and poverty, even after struggling so hard to be rich. Some people take on two jobs to be rich, working all through the seven days in the week. Yet the more they work, the more bills they have to pay, the more needs they have and the less abundance they live in.

Some have given up on the pursuit of living in abundance, because to them fate has not destined them to be rich. They are not among the lucky few who found favor with fate to live in abundance; hence, they better accept their fate and stop fighting what they cannot change. These sets of people have now come to believe that living in abundance is a matter of fate, favor and luck.

What an irony! Oh, how interesting will it be for you to know that you are the decider of your fate? How will you feel about knowing that a life of abundance or poverty is totally dependent on the choices you have made in life and your mindset about this area of your life? Will it shock you to know that you have the power to decide to be rich or poor? Will you believe that you have all it takes to live in abundance instead of poverty or will you live in disbelief because you think you have done all you can and it's left to fate to decide?

The truth still remains that God never created any of us to be poor. There is enough untapped, untouched and unused wealth on the earth to go round to everyone. But what you and I do with this great opportunity, I call "an open check" will determine what kind of life you and I will live on the earth.

What kind of life will you want to live; a life of poverty, a life of lack or a life of abundance? The choice is yours. God has given us all that pertain to life and living life to the fullest. Whatever kind of life you are living now is a direct result of your mindset, which is a product of what you know and what you don't know.

There is no shortage in the resources of the earth to make you live in abundance and plenty. The universe is full of opportunities that will offer you the kind of life you demand of it. You alone are the one standing between your desired kind of life and the life you are having right now.

How will life look like for you, if you were able to do whatever you wanted to do without money being a factor or limitation? Just pause and think about it for a minute. Can you begin to imagine what kind of serenity you will have when you are living a life of abundance and you don't have to worry about money but you are busy fulfilling your God given purpose? The Holy Book said it rightly, "MONEY ANSWERETH ALL THINGS".

In all the chapters of this book, you will discover the principles that those with the abundance mindset have that those with poverty mindset don't have. It is this knowledge that makes them lucky if there was anything like that. Instead of throwing in the towel, I will advise you put the knowledge from this book to work and watch as you begin to work into your luck, taking advantage of it and becoming financially free. Only those with poverty mindset leave their financial life and wellbeing in the hands of fate and others.

If you desire a life of abundance, if you are ready to discover how to begin to work towards living a life of abundance, if you are ready to create a life of abundance void of lack for yourself then continue reading this book, you are in a good company. However, if you want to be poor or live in lack, then this is not the book for you. You can discontinue reading this book at this moment because you are not in the right place. Surely this book will open your eyes to the abundance around you that you never took note of.

For those of us who would like to discover the principles to living the life of abundance and walk in it. Please, join me as we continue this beautiful journey to our desired destination. You too can be rich. Yes you can have and live a life of abundance!

LET THE JOURNEY BEGIN…!!!

PART 1

THE CAUSES OF POVERTY

CHAPTER 1

REAL POVERTY IS NOT IN THE SIZE OF YOUR POCKET BUT IN THE SIZE OF YOUR MIND

In many occasions when the topic of poverty is brought up, we tend to measure poverty by what someone has physically and what he doesn't have. But that is a very shallow estimation or description of what poverty is. Poverty is not determined by what you have and what you don't have. Poverty is rather a state of the mind. It is what you have in your mind or the size of your mind that determines the size of your pocket. The size of your mind is directly proportional to the size of your pocket. It is the content of your mind that determines the size of your pocket.

It really does not matter how dry and empty your pocket is, if you are wealthy in your mind soon your wealthy mind will reflect in your pocket. Money is not a determinant factor of who becomes rich or poor. It does not matter how much money you give to a man with a poverty mindset, he will still fall back into poverty it's just a matter of time. This explains what statistics show, that over 90% of all those who win huge amounts of money in lotteries go bankrupt after a few years.

For you to be rich, you have to be rich on the inside first. If not, if you eventually become rich on the outside without being rich on the inside, two things usually happen to people like this; they will lose their wealth or their wealth will destroy them. This is usually the case with must super stars who take to different kinds of drugs thereby losing their health and finally die.

When it comes to living in abundance or riches, your number one pursuit should not be how to make quick physical cash by any means possible. Let your number one pursuit be to invest in your mind. You are rich in your mind, if you enlarge the capacity of your mind with financial knowledge, there is no way the size of your pocket will be small or empty. Pay less attention to what you have in your pocket or what you don't have, concentrate on enlarging and enriching your mind with the right information, and before you know it, it will begin to reflect in your pocket.

OPPORTUNITY IS IN ABUNDANCE

Poverty is not a result of lack of opportunity, but rather lack of knowledge. Without knowledge, you cannot take advantage of an opportunity even when it stares at you. The cure to poverty therefore will not be to issue out money but to feed the mind with the necessary knowledge required for financial freedom. Charity has not made anyone rich. It has never in history turned a poor person from poverty to riches, or granted wealth to poor nations. Irrespective of how much third world nations receive on charity bases, none of these nations has ever moved from a third world nation to being a first world nation due to the amount they have received from charitable organizations. Rather they fall back into deeper debt. Charity to a great extent makes the poor comfortable in their poverty. Am I saying we should not be involved in charity, not at all. What I am rather saying is that to put a lasting end to poverty, the poor need their minds fed and not just their stomach.

If the mind can be filled with the right knowledge, there will be a shift in their mindset and poverty will be a thing of history. So the mind has to be properly developed and equipped with the necessary information, in order to have a shift from poverty to abundance. When the size of the pocket is small, our first area of focus should be the mind. This is the type of teachings that should be in our churches, schools, social groups and small groups, in order for us to be able to bring an end to poverty in our nation and continent at large.

There are several opportunities for riches today, but what we lack is a mind that can aid or enhance our physical eyes to see these opportunities and take advantage of them. For the life of abundance to be obtainable for a person, the mind has to be developed and equipped.

Have you ever wondered why two people will live in the same country, went to the same school, had same opportunities in life, and one will be rich while one is poor? The simple answer to these is yes. And the reason for it is the understanding of these two individuals. Don't forget that when it comes to understanding, the capacity of your mind determines how you understand and proffer solution to problems. Those who can see with the eyes of the mind can achieve greatness in life and live a life of abundance.

THE TWO SHOE SALES MEN

Two sales men from a competing shoe manufacturing companies where sent to Africa to assess the market for shoes. Though these two sales men were sent to the same country, had and saw the same circumstances, their perspectives however were totally different.

The first salesman scouts around for a few days and then heads for the telegraph office to contact the company headquarters. He writes: "Research complete. Unmitigated disaster! Nobody here wears shoes."

Likewise, the second salesman does his research and heads for the same telegraph office. Once there, he composes the following: "Research complete. Glorious opportunity! Nobody here wears shoes!"

The point, of course, is that Salesman two is the real entrepreneur, the person who sees opportunity where others do not. It is only the person that has the ability and understanding to see opportunity that can take advantage of it. And that can only be done with an enlarged mind. The capacity of the mind is what gives you the added advantage over others. It helps you to see potential, take risks and to turn obstacles into opportunities.

Of course salesman one packed his back and left the country, while sales man two persuaded his company into the production of cheap and affordable shoes. These he sold to the people and the company made several millions, so did he too. The question to you therefore is what can you see?

Most times I come across people that always complain about lack of money. I don't have money for this or that. I can't start my business, school etc. because I don't have money. That might just be the fact not the truth. The truth is that your mind is poor; you lack the power of creativity in your mind. That is why you are stuck. The problem is not money but the poverty of your mind. When you meet someone with a wealthy mind, you will not need to be told their mind is rich. They always have solution for every situation. Instead of complaining they find a way of carrying out their goals and dreams. They don't allow themselves to be stopped by the lack of money. Their creative mind often makes a way for them.

Our emphasis therefore should not be to meet the immediate seen need of the size of your pocket but rather we should pay greater attention to the unseen need, the size of the mind. If the size of the mind can be fixed, then there will be little or no problem with the size of the pocket. The universe is capable to provide abundance for everyone living. The problem therefore is not a question of if there is enough for all, but rather if the mind is capable of conceiving the abundance the universe had made available for all.

Empty pockets never held anyone back. Only empty heads and empty hearts can do that. (Norman Vincent Peale)

The reason therefore for lack is empty mind. If the mind can be filled with the needed information then the eyes can begin to see the vast opportunities that surround us on daily basis and can thereby take advantage of these opportunities. Instead of complaining of how nothing is working or how bad the economy is, ask yourself, what do I need to know in other to be able to take advantage of the seemingly bad economy? If there are people doing well in that economy, country, environment etc, then you do not have any excuse why you should not do well. You need to step out and seek knowledge. You need to know what they know that is making them do well in areas where you are failing.

EMPTY POCKET IS NOT THE PROBLEM

Your pocket might be empty today, but if your mind is filled up, then you are not poor. It is just a matter of time before your filled mind will cause your pocket to be filled up. When I am talking about filled mind or getting your mind filled up with the right information, I am not talking about school education, or going to get a college degree. That is not in any way bad, but that is not what will give you the right information that will raise you above poverty. What do I mean by that? College education alone is not enough to make anyone rich. I will discuss this in details in subsequent chapters of this book.

You need financial knowledge. That is what your mind needs to be filled with. You need to know the laws of money in order to know how money works. If you do not know how money works, it does not matter how many degrees you have, you will never live or enjoy financial freedom, talk more of living in abundance. You will remain a perpetual slave to pay check. The more you work the more needs you have, the more tax you pay then the more you need to work again. You get entrapped into the pay check web because of the smallness of your mind.

If you really want to move a person from poverty to riches, you don't need to give them money. That shouldn't be the first approach. Don't fill their pockets when you have not filled their minds. Filling their pocket and leaving their minds empty is to push them into greater level of poverty or at its best give them comfort in poverty. The only thing that can move a poor man from poverty to a life of permanent riches is having the size of his mind enlarged to a great capacity. When the mind is filled up, a man will not need charity or lottery to have his pocket filled up. If at this point money is given, he will have the capacity to multiply that which has being given to him and increase in his wealth acquisition.

Before you give the poor money, give them knowledge that is if you want to pull them out of poverty except your agenda is to push them into further or deeper level of poverty, then you can give them all the money to fill their pockets and leave their minds empty.

When you give people money that they are not prepared for, they will lose it at its best or the money will ruin them and snatch life out of them because they do not have the necessary capacity required to handle the huge amount of money given. Let's take a look at what statistics have to say about lottery winners.

According to a 2010 study by researchers at Vanderbilt University, the University of Kentucky and the University of Pittsburgh, the more money you win in the lottery, the more likely you are to end up bankrupt.

The authors divided past lottery winners into two separate groups: Those who had won cash prizes between $50,000 and $150,000, and those who had won $10,000 or less. What they found is that those who had won the more sizable sums were more likely to have filed for bankruptcy five years later. Similar research from the National Endowment for Financial Education estimates that 70 percent of people who had unexpectedly come into large sums of money ended up broke within seven years. Take for example the following cases

Callie Rogers:

Britain's youngest-ever lottery winner wasted away the money on drugs, booze and cosmetic surgery. She became so depressed, she even (allegedly) attempted suicide three times. Rogers was introduced to cocaine by a boyfriend and spent over $400,000 on the drug in six years before getting clean. She also got breast implants, fancy cars and more.

Rogers was so broke, she could not even afford to have favorite gift for just 99 cents! Now that Rogers is broke, she's back home living with her parents and works as a maid.

William "Bud" Post:

You would think winning the lottery for $16.2 million would be a dream come true. But like almost every other case, it soon turned into hell on earth. William "Bud" Post had just $2.46 in his bank account. He just finished serving 28 days in prison.

To afford lottery ticket, Post sold a ring for $40 and purchased 40 lotto tickets. Two weeks after winning, Post went on a spending spree... spending more than $300,000 on buying a restaurant, a used-car lot and an airplane. William "Bud" Post died 18 years after his big win. He admitted he was both careless and foolish, trying to please his family. He eventually declared bankruptcy and died over a million dollars in debt. He allegedly remarked that "I was much happier when I was broke."

I have decided to add these two examples out of several others, just to buttress my point on the real cause of poverty being the size of the mind and not the pocket. A bigger pocket will only amount to more problems and causes of deeper or worst poverty for those with little minds. It is therefore expedient to focus more on the size of the mind and less on the size of the pocket when your course is to the fight against poverty. Selah!

GOLDEN NUGGETS

1. Poverty is not necessarily a function of what you have or don't have in your pocket.
2. The main cause of poverty is a function of the mind
3. A rich pocket with an empty mind leads to destruction
4. Poverty is not a function of the your country of origin
5. Every country has the rich and poor.
6. Poverty is not just a function of a poor economy or bad politicians
7. Before you give the poor money give them knowledge.
8. Charity has not made any nation financially free
9. What the poor need is not money but financial knowledge.
10. A full mind is the cure to an empty pocket
11. If there is but one person rich in your neighborhood, then you don't have excuse for poverty.
12. Poverty is a state of the mind

CHAPTER 2
IGNORANCE IS THE NUMBER ONE CAUSE OF POVERTY

Well, it is very interesting how we like to play the blame game when it comes to the issues of poverty and lack. We have several hundreds of reasons why we are poor and not rich. You ask some people to make their list why they are not rich, you will be dumb-founded at the several reasons people have. Everyone seems to have a reason why they are not successful. But one major thing is usually missing from this list. That is "I". I am yet to see anyone who has accepted that they are the reason for their poverty. No one will like to accept this or take the responsibility for the state they find themselves in. In order to be able to cause a change, you must be ready to take responsibility.

> *I know that government doesn't have the all solutions that real solutions do not come from the top down. Instead, the ways to end poverty come from all of us. We are part of the solution. (Governor Kathleen Blanco)*

We blame our government, politicians, the economy, inflation, etc. Nigerians to a large extent and Africans at large are plagued with the habit of playing the blame game. We find it very difficult to take responsibilities for our difficulties and financial adversities. Some people even go to the extent of blaming the rich. Isn't that ridiculous? Yes it is! But that is what we do. As much as there might be some facts to this blame game, as much as the government, the economy, might have a part in this, but that is not the whole truth. It is just a fact. The major cause or should I say the number one cause of poverty is ignorance. You are the one keeping yourself in poverty. It is your ignorance that is holding you back. Your lack of financial knowledge has become like a strong chain that bound you to a life of perpetual poverty and lack.

If you doubt me, let me make the analysis clear to you. This is usually my argument when I meet with people that claim the system of their country is against them that is why they cannot be rich. If you fall into this category of people, my number one question to you will be this, are there people in your country or in the same system as you that are successful? If the answer is yes, then you do not have any argument. Because if one person has been able to do something, it means it can be done and someone else can do it. All that is needed is to get to know the principle by which it was done.

"What one man can do, another can do." (from the movie "THE EDGE")

So your complaints of the government and bad economy being the reason for your poverty does not hold water if there is but one person that is rich in that same environment. Inflation could not possibly be holding you back when there are other rich fellows in your neighborhood. Why should you be among the people the government, bad economy, inflation etc. are holding back from being rich, instead of being among those who are rich despite all these factors surrounding them? The simple answer is ignorance!

26

To let you know how ignorance can really subject you to living a life of poverty while sitting on diamond, I will like you to meet Joana. Joana was an elderly woman living in a two room mud house then in a village in one of the western countries in Africa. She could barely eat three square means. She had a little farm where she cultivates and goes to the bush to pick palm nuts which she breaks and sells as a means of income. There was this large stone she inherited from her parents on which she breaks these palm nuts and gets out the kernels. This stone was covered with dirt as it has been with her for decades.

One faithful day during the colonization, some British business men came to this part of the country, saw this stone and had knowledge of what it was. They told the woman that they will build her a four bed room bungalow in exchange for the stone. Her joy knew no bounds as she was wondering what in the world these men were going to do with an old stone. She went into agreement with them and was so excited and perplexed at their generosity according to her, "Generosity indeed"

Well they went through with their agreement with her; built her the house and she gave them the stone in exchange. These men went back with the large stone to England and discovered that they were right with their speculations. The large stone was a diamond, the purest form of diamond they have ever come in contact with, in its raw state. These men, out of this business deal with this woman became multimillionaires in British Pounds.

*Poverty has many roots, but
the tap root is ignorance.
(Lyndon B Johnson)*

Even though this woman had this diamond for decades, she could not take any advantage of it because of ignorance. To her this large piece of diamond was only but a stone. A stone on which she breaks palm nuts to make ends meet. This is how must people still live today in their day to day activity while blaming the rich, government, economy, nation etc. for the cause of their poverty. If you must overcome poverty you must seek knowledge. Not just knowledge but financial knowledge.

You have to step out of your comfort zone to go and seek for financial knowledge. Learn from those who are beating the system you are in. What do they know that you don't know, that is making them succeed where you and others are failing? That will be the beginning of your deliverance from poverty. But as long as you just sit down there and complain about what is against you and how your country is bad, poverty will make your home its dwelling place.

MY COUNTRY IS POOR

Let me let you know, that poverty or riches is never a function of your country of origin or a factor of the country you are based in. A lot of people believe this, especially people from the developing countries, Africans and Nigerians to be precise. But that is a big myth and misconception of the highest order. Every country in the world comprises of the poor and the rich irrespective of how developed that nation is. Let's take for example the present world power, the United States of America. I know so many people will want to run to America in order to have a better life and escape poverty. But that is deception. Some will even say things like, if I can only get to America, all my problems will be over. This is another big sign of ignorance in the highest order.

It might interest you to know that the percentage of the rich to the poor in American is about 90 to 10; 90% poor, 10% rich. Does that shock you? Well, it is the truth. There are so many homeless and dejected people in America than you can even count. So many people, who are enslaved to their jobs working like horses, yet cannot make ends meet. This does not apply to only America but every other country in the world. I only used America as an example because that is where most people want to run to today in order to have the American dream.

Take a look at these statistics: It's important to make a distinction between income and wealth because income inequality and wealth inequality aren't equal. According to research originally done by economists Thomas Piketty and Emmanuel Saez, the top 1 percent of income earners took home 17.67 percent of the total income -- less than a fifth -- of everyone in the U.S in 2008 [source: Alvaredo et al]. To qualify as the top 1 percent of earners, you need to make a little more than $500,000 in cash income in 2011 [source: Rampell].

Wealth inequality is far greater. According to an analysis of Federal Reserve data by the Economic Policy Institute, the wealthiest 1 percent of Americans control 35.6 percent of the total wealth of the country -- more than a third [source: Allegretto]. Even more incredible is that the richest 10 percent of Americans control 75 percent of the wealth, leaving only 25 percent to the other 90 percent of Americans.

Every country has both the poor and the rich. Running from one country to the other, is not a solution to poverty. Neither does it change who you are. The only change it can bring to you is moving you from an insignificant poor man to a glorified poor man. Smiles, that's if you get what I mean. The only thing that can change you is a shift in your mindset which comes through knowledge. The moment the right knowledge comes in, ignorance gives way and the light that comes with knowledge shines on the darkness of poverty, eradicating it. Then and only then will riches begin to flow into your pocket, and you say farewell to poverty.

Now that you know that poverty or riches is not a function of the country you live in, I suggest that instead of you running from "pillar to post" looking for greener pastures, you should seek knowledge. Replace your ignorance with knowledge. When I am talking about acquiring knowledge in this book, I am in no way talking about going to school to get a degree. As much as that is very important, college degree will not make you rich. I will talk more on that in subsequent chapters in this book.

So go seek financial knowledge from those who are already successful. Learn the game of the rich. Learn the laws and principles of money and prosperity. It is only sound financial knowledge input that can put an end to poverty and financial slavery. Do you wish for financial freedom? Then get adequate financial knowledge.

Most times we lay so much emphasis on education, and when we talk about education, it is usually about going to school to get one degree or the other. Let me make this clear, a degree is not the solution or an answer to the problem of poverty. Like I said earlier and I will also deal with that in details in subsequent chapters. We have to understand that not all knowledge is relevant to a particular course. So as much as we will seek knowledge, it is very important that we seek appropriate knowledge that can be effective, in providing solutions to the causes of poverty. And also giving a direction towards the world of riches that is available to everyone on planet earth but very few have the opportunity of working in that path and enjoying the vast resources the universe has made available.

In this chapter, I have been talking about ignorance as the cause of poverty in our time. To fully understand this, I will like us to get to really know what ignorance is, so we can get out of its web.

Ignorance means having a lack of information or lack of knowledge. It is different from stupidity which is lack of intelligence and different from foolishness which is lack of wisdom. The three are often mixed up and assumed to be the same by some people.

"Knowledge is power," goes the old saying. Unfortunately, some people, knowing this, try to keep knowledge to themselves (as a strategy of obtaining an unfair advantage), and hinder others from obtaining knowledge. Do not expect that if you train someone in a particular skill, or provide some information, that the information or skill will naturally trickle or leak into the rest of a community.

It is important to determine what the information is, that is missing. Many planners and good minded persons, who want to help a community become stronger, think that the solution is education. But education means many things, some information may not be important to the situation at hand. It will not help a farmer to know that Romeo and Juliet both died in Shakespeare's play, but it would be more useful to know which kind of seed would survive in the local soil, and which would not.

What do I mean by this, as much as acquiring knowledge is important, we must seek to acquire knowledge that is relevant to the course we are pursuing. In most cases, the knowledge we need to move from poverty is not found in our different schools or colleges. What we need to know, is how money works, the principles of wealth creation and the laws of money. To be financially free, just generalized knowledge is not enough. What we need is specified knowledge.

Unfortunately most of our schools don't handle these topics, as most of the lecturers or teachers that train students in the different schools are not financially free themselves. It is impossible to give what you don't have. Neither does the school curriculum make provision for such training. So as individuals, in addition to your school education, you have to pursue self-education. It is self-education that holds the key to your financial freedom.

Just has Jim Rohn rightly said:

"Formal education will make you a living; self-education will make you a fortune"

Get to meet those who know how money works, those who are financially free themselves and learn what they know. After you have gotten the knowledge, begin to apply it in your own life. Only by so doing will you get a lasting result, which is living above the claws of poverty and lack in a rich world.

TAKE RESPONSIBILITY FOR YOUR FINANCIAL STATUS

I want you as an individual to take personal responsibility for your financial status. Do not leave this vital part of your live in the hands of the government, economy, your country etc. stop playing the blame game and start looking for the loop holes in your life that have stopped you from having enough and living in lack in a world full of plenty. You don't need to be angry with the rich or blame the rich for your lack. Rather make friends with them to learn what they know that you don't know. Always remember that whatsoever you do not admire and appreciate, you cannot acquire. Your problem is not the rich, politicians, your government or country. Your number one problem is your ignorance. You are your own problem. If you therefore must be rich then you must be ready to face these facts and deal with them from the grass root.

Remember, for there to be any change in your life circumstances, you must change. You must improve yourself. You must develop your mind. You must change your company. If you want to fly like the eagles, then you have to make friends with the Eagles and not with chickens. You can't be in the company of chickens and hope to fly like the Eagles someday. Life does not work that way.

You will be the same person in five years as you are today except for the people you meet and the books you read. (Charlie Jones)

Pursue the right knowledge, read the right book, meet the right people. Well, you might want to ask, how can I know the right knowledge to pursue, the right book to read, and the right people to meet? It's quite simple. Only listen to those who have been able to achieve what you are pursuing. Those are the kind of people you can get the right knowledge from, read their books and make friends with them if possible. For no one in the real sense of it can give what they do not have. I personally do not believe a man has knowledge of something, if that knowledge is not productive in his own life.

It will be ridiculous to go and seek financial wisdom from a person who is bankrupt, wouldn't it? But that is what we do most of the time. If I want financial freedom, then I have to go to someone who is financially free to seek knowledge on how to be financially free. I won't go to a salary earner to seek such wisdom. Many people rely on their banks for their financial education and knowledge, without realizing that over 90% of our so called banks are not financially free. Neither do they know how to be financially free.

Some people rely on their stock brokers, but 95% of stock brokers are not financially free themselves. The right people to seek knowledge from when it comes to financial freedom should be those who have attained that height themselves. Be smart, don't fall into that trap. Take the decision to kiss poverty goodbye, by taking the very first step of acquiring the right knowledge from the right people. Never be reluctant to learn new things. Don't be so comfortable in your old ways that have proven to be unproductive or that have kept you in financial bondage. Say no to ignorance, and the days of poverty in your life will gradually come to an end.

Learning is the beginning of wealth. Learning is the beginning of health. Learning is the beginning of spiritually. Searching and learning is where the miracle process all begins. The great Breakthrough in your life comes when you realize it that you can learn anything you need to learn to accomplish any goal that you set for yourself. This means there are no limits on what you can be, have or do. (Unknown)

GOLDEN NUGGETS
● ● ● ● ● ● ● ● ● ● ● ● ● ●

1. You and you alone decide your financial status.

2. Stop playing the blame game and begin to take responsibility for your financial life.

3. The government is not your problem

4. Ignorance is the mother of your financial lack

5. Stop running from pillar to post. There is no country that guarantees financial freedom.

6. Lack of financial knowledge is the major reason for poverty.

7. Financial knowledge is different from educational knowledge.

8. Go seek knowledge from those who have attained financial freedom.

9. If one person can do it, you can do it. There is no excuse for poverty.

10. For your circumstance to change, you have to change.

11. The rich is not your problem.

12. If you want to know the cause of your financial lack, please take a look at the mirror

Chapter 3
IT IS WHAT WE DON'T KNOW THAT IS KILLING US

As much as we will not like to admit to this truth, it still does not change it from being the truth. It is what we don't know that is killing us. There is no way you can live better without knowing better. The standard of our living is directly proportional to our knowledge. The reason for the rampant spread of poverty is lack of knowledge. It is a total disservice to education, how our school curriculums have been programmed. We are taught different things in school except for this very important facet of it.

No school today teaches about prosperity and how you can be rich; no school teaches the principles of money. Students are rather trained and equipped to become perpetual workers for money thereby remaining a slave to their work and living in poverty. The difference between those who have an abundance mindset and those who have poverty mindset is what they know.

The churches in Nigeria have rather multiplied the problem of financial ignorance. Instead of the church teaching the congregation and the masses at large about financial laws and principles, they have rather multiplied the problem by dishing out erroneous teachings that have led to more people ending in poverty and enlarging the pockets of the pastors. They have taught the people that giving is what brings financial prosperity and God's favor, thereby making the people live in superstitions, while poverty keeps spreading and ravaging them.

To stop the spread of poverty, we must then begin to spread the financial knowledge. We must concentrate on changing the mindset of the people with the right information instead of focusing on changing the size of the pocket of the poor. What the poor need the most is not food or charity. As much as this is important, the number one need of the poor is information. They need the right financial knowledge on how to turn their situation around. As much as it might sound good to give a man fish to satisfy his hunger, I believe it is best to teach a man to fish and prevent him from going hungry in the first place. A man that knows how to fish will not need to wait for anyone to bring him fish.

> *You can't get rid of poverty by giving*
> *people money.*
> *(P.J. O'Rourke)*

So many people have been killed financially because of what they don't know about finances. So many people have gone from riches to rags, from grace to grass because of lack of adequate knowledge about money. What bewilders me the most is why such a relevant topic that affects every area of life is not being address in our colleges and schools. When I hear people talk about money, I discover how much most educated people are ignorant when it comes to the principles of money. The wrong concepts are being promoted in our society today.

28 years old Tony was the only child of his rich parents. Even though Tony was from a rich home, he knew little or nothing concerning the laws of money. He always got what he wanted from his parents and they never had time to teach him about the principles of money.

On this fateful day, Tony's parents were involved in an auto mobile accident that claimed their lives, leaving all their wealth and estate to the management of Tony. It was not up to ten years after their death, Tony went bankrupt. He lacked financial knowledge and engaged mostly in buying liabilities he thought were assets. Within a short period of time the money and riches developed wings and flew away from Tony. Money will always move from the hands of the ignorant to the hands of the knowledgeable.

We need to go out of our way to seek this knowledge for ourselves. We cannot leave our lives in the hands of any other human being on earth. We have to take our lives into our hands, by going out to seek financial knowledge from those who know and begin to put it to work. That is exactly what this book will do for you. It will provide you with the necessary knowledge you need to stay afloat in your finances as you climb the ladder of success. You are in good company reading this book.

If you will not get any other thing from this chapter, I want you to get this one thing, hold up to it and always remember, that it is not your government that is killing you, it is not the economy or inflation that is killing you neither is it your country of origin or residence. What is killing you is what you do not know. We have been dished a lot of financial and investment balderdash, that would not in any way help us annihilate poverty from our lives and homes.

Most of the things you have been taught that are assets, are actually a well packaged liability. We have to unlearn in order to be able to relearn the vital truths of the laws of money, investments, assets and liabilities. Until we know these fundamentals, we are still going to be killed by what we don't know, while we continue in our circle of the blame game. So please stay with me till the end of this book and you will be making these amazing discoveries for yourself. But you have to make a commitment to put the knowledge you get from this book into practice.

GOLDEN NUGGETS

1. It is what we don't know that is killing us.
2. Our standard of living is directly proportional to our level of knowledge.
3. Lack of knowledge is the reason for poverty.
4. To stop the spread of poverty, we have to spread knowledge
5. Charity is not a cure to poverty.
6. A change mindset will result to a change in the size of the pocket.
7. Ignorantly mistaking liabilities for assets
8. We can't live better without knowing better.
9. It is better to teach a man to fish than to give him fish
10. Stop playing the blame game
11. Take responsibility for your financial life
12. Our schools do not teach us how to be financially free

CHAPTER 4

NEVER TAKE ADVICE FROM THOSE WHO ARE IGNORANT OF THE LAWS OF MONEY

You need to be very careful of who you take advice from when it comes to the issues of finance. So many people who present themselves as financial advisers know little or nothing about the laws of money. Majority of the people we look up to for financial advice, have a very superficial knowledge which is not balanced when it comes to the laws of money.

Just because someone works in the bank or let's say someone is a banker, does not mean he or she has any appropriate knowledge of the laws of money. The worst thing you can do to your financial future is to surround yourself with people who call themselves financial advisers but know so little or nothing about finance.

Stock brokers are not always the best people to take financial advice from. Just like Robert Kiyosaki quoted his rich dad in his book, Rich Dad Poor Dad; "they are called brokers because they are more broke than you are". That someone has a degree in finance or banking, does not in any way suggest that they are knowledgeable when it comes to the principles and laws of money. You have to therefore be careful of who you listen to when it comes to this area of life. Because so many people you even hold in high esteem are ignorant about the laws of money.

> *Wall Street is the only place that people ride to in a Rolls-Royce to get advice from those who take the subway. (Warren Buffett)*

Your parents are not always the best people to take financial advice from, except they are vast in the knowledge of the principles and laws of money, this should always be determined by their track record. Yes of a truth, your parents mean well for you, but that they mean well for you does not mean they are always right. Which simply means someone can have good intentions and still be very wrong. Good intentions are not in any way equivalent to knowledge. Before you get very sentimental and carried away by what seems to be right, double check the advice you are being given and who is giving it.

Mr. Jones met an untimely death as a result of wrong advice from a financial adviser. Mr. Jones was a prosperous business man who was doing well for himself until he made one of the make money fast investments. A deal was brought to him to make an investment in a line of business he knew very little about. However he was motivated to go into this business because of the huge returns the business promised. The deal looked very attractive indeed but that was only on the superficial level.

Mr. Jones therefore decided to meet with another investor to advise him on this deal, who confirmed it was a great area to invest in, out of so much excitement Mr. Jones did not do his due diligence anymore to check all the pros and cons before moving ahead with the investment. He trusted the advice he got from this investor and the inquiries he made from his financial adviser.

Owing to the fact that this investment was so huge, Mr. Jones did not have all the necessary capital required. So after diverting all his resources to this investment, he still went to the bank to take loans to invest in this deal using his house and landed properties as collaterals for them. He was so excited believing that in a matter of months he was going to be a multimillionaire. Little did he know that the months ahead were going to be his days of disaster.

In conclusion, the deal failed, and Mr. Jones lost all he has labored for all his life in a matter of months. As if this was not bad enough, the banks were going to come for his landed properties and his house leaving him homeless. Mr. Jones could not handle the devastation that has just met him from nowhere without any sign or previous warnings. He had a cardiac arrest and before they could get him medical attention he died. These are the kinds of losses and pains that come with taking advice from the wrong person or source. Be careful who you listen to on financial issues.

To be on the safe side, I will advise you take your financial advice from people who know the principles and the laws of money. The next question will be how do I know those who know the laws of money? It is very simple to know, all you need to do is find people that are rich, not just every rich person but those that became rich from their efforts and investments. Not people who got money by inheritance or those who won the lottery, but those who are rich and their wealth are growing constantly by virtue of their investment, knowledge and hard work. Have you ever heard that saying; you cannot give what you do not have? Well that is also true in this sphere of life.

How can you possibly be a financial adviser when you are struggling in poverty yourself? You are living from paycheck to paycheck, and you want me to listen to you? No, if you know as much as you claim you know, then put your knowledge to work, let it work for you, only then will I or should you be comfortable learning or taking advice from them.

Are you familiar with those popular advices from parents? Go to school, work hard, get a college degree so you can get a good paying job, with insurance and financial freedom. What a superficial advice? Do you really think anyone can be financially free just by having a good paying job? No I don't think so. These are one of those numerous advices that have put a lot of people in financial bondage, making them a slave to their jobs. It is impossible to be living from paycheck to paycheck and have financial freedom.

Wall Street is the only place that people ride to in a Rolls-Royce to get advice from those who take the subway. (Warren Buffett)

When it comes to the issue of financial freedom, everyone seems to have something to say, or some sort of advice to give. My question then is how many people are living in financial freedom in our world today? Over 80% of the world population is under financial slavery, so you can see how risky it is for you to take financial advice from everyone you see, just because they dress well, drive a good car and call themselves financial advisers. You want to double check any advice and the person giving the advice before you consider it. If it is not at work in the life of the person, forget about it.

It is more like going to a sales person to ask him if he thinks you should buy the product he is selling. What do you think will be his response? Of course he will advise you to buy. Well as long as that sales person is concerned at that moment, his product is going to be the best available in the market.

Never ask a barber if you need a haircut.
(Warren Buffet)

Always remember this, never be in a hurry to buy anything you are pressurized and persuaded so much to buy, if you do, you might just be buying the wrong thing or making the wrong investment. Do your due diligence by seeking the right people to take financial advice from. Don't forget, the best advice you can get is from those who are financially free themselves. Surround yourself with the right people and you will sure be on your way to making right choices.

GOLDEN NUGGETS

• • • • • • • • • • • • • •

1. Be careful of who you take financial advice from.

2. Financial literacy is not tied to job or professional description.

3. Just because someone is a banker does not mean they know the laws of money.

4. When it comes to financial issues, your parents are not always the best to take advice from except they have proven track record.

5. Most people you hold in high esteem are ignorant of the laws of money.

6. To be on the safe side, only take financial advice from those who are financially free.

7. No one can give what they don't have

8. Good intention does not always equate to being right

9. Someone may have good intentions and be totally wrong.

10. Your parents always mean well for you but that does not mean they always have the right financial advice.

11. Double check every advice and the person giving it before implementing them.

12. If their advice is not at work in their life, don't listen to them.

CHAPTER 5

LACK OF INTEREST TO LEARN NEW THINGS

We are living in a fast pace world today. A lot of things are changing by the second. During the last century we have moved from the Industrial Age through the Information Age to the Knowledge Age. The ability to obtain, assimilate and apply the right knowledge effectively will become a key skill in the next century. Our ability will no longer be judged solely by qualifications gained in the past, but will also be assessed by our capacity to learn and adapt in the future.

Learning isn't just about economic success. However, it is the key to achieving our full potential. Human beings are uniquely adapted to learn and we have the ability to do so throughout our lives. Learning has the power to transform us. Specifically, we can become more successful. We have metamorphosed from the Stone Age to industrial age and now the information age. For us to be able to keep up with the pace of our time, we have to be ready to continually learn new things. You have to be conversant with the new way of doing things. If not sooner or later, you will be out of business or left behind.

There was a time when driving was a big deal. Most people didn't know how to drive, and those who knew how to drive (drivers) made huge money out of that profession. But today the reverse is the case. Almost everyone owns a car and can drive. The driving occupation is no longer needed today as much as it was 20-30years ago. That is why in this present time, you must have more than one skill and be ready to be a constant student in order to remain relevant in our world today. You must never allow yourself to be lazy in your mind. You have to work harder on your mind than on your job.

New invention comes up every day that causes the value of the old one to be depreciated. There was a time, when typing machine was a big deal and we had those who made typing an occupation. Every office seemed to have a typing machine then and a typist. But today there is no occupation as such. No office today goes in search of a typist, neither is the typewriter in use in most offices anymore. That is the power of new things. The only thing that is permanent in life is change. If you must stay relevant, then you must be up to date with the new ways of doing things, new inventions and a current knowledge of technology.

As a matter of fact, we are living in an age of technology. To be vast and effective, basic knowledge of technology is needed. You need to equip yourself with the necessary skill needed to be able to compete in the market place. Without this basic knowledge and skills, your value will be reduced. Alvin Toffler said it rightly:

"The illiterate of the 21st century will not be those who cannot read and write, but those who cannot learn, unlearn, and relearn."

I totally agree with Alvin Toffler on this one. Constant learning, relearning and unlearning is a must for the achievement of success today. The knowledge and teachings that were handed down to us from our parents are no longer effective today in most cases. Remember the popular advice of going to school, work hard, get a good job and save in order to be financially free? Well, that advice is no longer applicable today, as most of the present day financially free people are not those who had some college degrees or were they the best students in their schools.

The question now is what is now applicable in our time? What are the things that lead to financial freedom in our time? What is the role of thump for today? Those are the things we are going to look at in subsequent chapters in this book. You have to be open minded, ready to learn, relearn and unlearn.

For instance, in our world today, you have to be able to use a computer. So the basic knowledge of computer is very relevant. You have to have an email and know how to operate one. Gone are the days we totally depended on the post office to post our mails. You have to be able to use the internet and source for relevant information you might need online. Without this basic knowledge, you will be greatly limited.

So it is with every sphere of life. Irrespective of your occupation, specialization, talents and skill you must be ready and willing to constantly learn new things in order to stay relevant. You can't just be dependent on your past achievement or a degree or skill you acquired in the past. Learning should be progressive especially today in this 21st century.

SEVEN ADVANTAGES OF LEARNING SOMETHING NEW

1. It will help you to grow constantly as a person, develop your knowledge base and improve

yourself for the better.

2. Learning something new gets us access to new and different opportunities and the chance to try new experiences that might be the best ones you have ever tried!

3. You could potentially earn more money in your work life from learning a new and appropriate skill or by developing one that links to the work you do. You'll rejuvenate your working life and get so much more from it.

4. Developing a new skill will influence the way you do things day to day and they will make doing things quicker and easier, saving time, energy and stress.

5. Learning across our lives is essential for staying up to date in an ever-changing world. If we stop learning things, we can stagnate and actually move backwards, especially in our professional lives.

6. Learning new things is very important for our self-esteem. Learning something new keeps brain cells active and allows us to succeed at something new, allowing us to give ourselves a big pat on the back!

7. Trying anything different ensures you meet new people, some of whom will have similar interests as you and be interested in some of the same things. You could make new friends and really enhance your social or work life.

It is so important to try new things and push yourself out of your comfort zone. The potential benefits are really huge and to be honest, there is nothing to lose, so you should start today and learn something new! Just this singular act will add so many flavors to your life, career, skills and your overall value in the market place.

GOLDEN NUGGETS

1. Be willing to always learn something new.
2. Learning should be a lifestyle
3. Acquire new skills
4. We are living in a fast pace world.
5. Change is the only thing that is permanent.
6. Don't be ashamed to learn something new.
7. Developing new skills will affect the way you do things daily.
8. Constant learning is the key to achieving our full potential.
9. If you want to be financially free, then you must be a constant student.
10. Push yourself to learn something new in other to stay relevant.
11. Those with better skills do better in the market place
12. Stay on top of your game.

PART 2

FACTORS THAT LEAD TO POVERTY

CHAPTER 6
THE LOVE TO REMAIN IN COMFORT ZONE

It is a fact that we all at one point or the other are comfortable in some areas of our life that we might not want to let go of or change. It is also true, that some of us are so tied to our comfort zones that we will never try anything that will try to push us from our comfort zone. As much as I understand how much you love your comfort zone, and how much you don't want to change, it is rather unfortunate, because change is the only thing that is constant in life.

One thing the rich know and embrace that the poor shrink from is the ability to step out of the comfort zone. The rich know how to put themselves in a place of temporal discomfort to achieve their goal, while the poor do not love to leave their comfort zone. The rich do not allow the fear of testing new waters stop them from doing it, they will rather do it. While the poor settle for their comfort zone to avoid the unknown thereby living in the fear of the unknown. Fear has crippled more destinies than disasters.

No one ever became wealthy doing only what they are comfortable with. For you to be wealthy, you have to learn to take a leap of faith that will definitely throw you out of your comfort zone. You have to learn to take risk in other to get to your desired goal. If you do not push yourself from your comfort zone then you will live in discomfort for the rest of your life. But those who subject themselves to a temporal discomfort to achieve their goal will have the opportunity to live a life of comfort in plenty for the rest of their lives.

For you to be able to achieve anything worthwhile in life, you must learn to leave your place of comfort or better still be open to those great challenges that will throw you out of your comfort zone. That is the greatest and fastest way to grow you can ever think of. It will hurt but in it you will have great gain.

Those who love comfort zones never take risks. And those who never take risks are not great achievers. Everyone you see in life, read about, or you hear has done anything tangible or extraordinary, check their life and study them, they were always risk takers. Those who will be ready to step out to pursue their dreams without knowing what their dream holds in stock for them. They are the ones that are not afraid of failure. No matter how many times they fail, they rise up and keep pushing forward until they achieve their goals. Trying not to risk anything and remaining in your comfort zone is the greatest risk of all, for life is a risk. To live to our full capacity, we have to learn to take reasonable risks and step out of our comfort zone.

The greatest risk is to risk nothing at all. (Leo Buscaglia)

Choosing to risk nothing is the greatest risk of all. When you are afraid of risking, you lose out on a lot of great opportunities in life. It is vital for us to step out to find out the opportunities life has made available to us on all angles. We cannot be our best at our comfort zone. We cannot have financial freedom by just sticking to what we know. We have to be ready to taste new waters and take advantage of the opportunities that come our way.

Most of the great opportunities life will bring our way are not always in the area of our comfort zone. It is vital to know different areas and ways of approaching different opportunities, in order to be able to make the best out of the opportunity. Don't be too rigid and stagnant. Learn to be open-minded to different opportunities and take the time to study the new opportunities and try to make the best of them.

It is high time you got out of the comfort zone of the deceptive teachings of prosperity going on in the churches today. Teachings that make you believe you can get something for nothing, waiting and hoping for the wonderful miracle of God that will bring you into the riches you desire. Living in the deception of having financial prosperity just by giving, you have to understand that life is lived based on principles not miracles.

What Is A Comfort Zone?

Comfort zone: the level at which one functions with ease and familiarity

Your comfort zone is the physical and mental space where your activities do not stress your routine. It is the place where there is less resistance, stress and risk. It provides a space that offers security, peace, less stress, minimized anxiety and maximized happiness.

Each day offers new experiences. Our ability to embrace changes in those opportunities influences how quickly we succeed or fail. In other words, it is necessary to be comfortably uncomfortable. The feelings created in this discomfort are often highly stressful; however, the rewards are even higher.

Nothing worthwhile has ever been ac-complished with a guarantee of success.
(John F. Kennedy)

SOME ADVANTAGES OF LEAVING YOUR COMFORT ZONE

- Change becomes easier – No one thinks change is easy, but the more you learn to accept the challenge of change, the easier it becomes to step into the uncomfortable space outside your comfort zone. Looking at change as a challenge gives it a whole new meaning. It is a challenge to succeed!

- Increased creativity – Everything within your comfort zone is not only comfortable, but you've experienced it before. When you try new things, see new things and do new things, your creativity is sparked and you start to think new things. The imagination has more fuel, so your thoughts are fresh and new.

- Talents/skills are honed – By experiencing new and exciting things outside your comfort zone, not only do you find new things that you enjoy do-ing, but you also discover what you're really good at doing. Knowing what you like and what you're good at is wonderful knowledge that enables you to cultivate your true talents.

- Know yourself – Stepping outside your comfort zone enables you to get to know the real you. Not only do you discover the things that you are good at doing, but you also learn what you enjoy and don't enjoy doing. Basically, you get to know yourself.

- Confidence increases – Each time you step out of your comfort zone and succeed in your adventure, your confidence in yourself and your abilities increase. When in doubt, you begin to find it easier to believe yourself.

- Increased focus/concentration – When outside your comfort zone, you usually have heightened awareness and sensitivities. This overload of sights, sounds and experiences enables you to also focus more clearly on the things that matter the most to you.

- You have more control – Eventually there will be reasons that you have to move outside your comfort zone. Why not make sure that you choose when, where and how you enter that uncomfortable area? Although you will have the same feelings of stress, but if forced into the comfort zone, you will feel even more stress.

- Increased growth – No one can grow in a vacuum. Outside of your comfort zone new experiences are waiting and that means growth possibilities. For instance, if you already know how to drive a car, getting into a car and driving doesn't offer any new or exciting possibilities. Stepping out of your comfort zone and getting into a race car going 200 mph across the Nevada desert would definitely offer you an opportunity for growth. It may also make you scared out of your mind.

- Self-trust – Once you step outside your comfort zone and know your boundaries, it is so much easier to trust yourself. You know what you can and can't safely or easily do. You know what you're good at and can accomplish with ease. Trusting yourself is not only necessary, but brings about peace.

- Self-worth/self-esteem is increased – Knowing that you can successfully meet challenges and new experiences gives you a boost in self-esteem. Not only do you feel more accomplished and able to meet challenges head on, but you feel that you add value to those you love and the world. With each success outside your comfort zone, you are more prone to feel better about yourself.

- Add value to the world – When we improve our self, we are improving the world around us.

- Accomplish goals faster – Outside your comfort zone with the uncomfortableness of not knowing everything and being shrouded with newness, it is easier to accomplish goals because your mind is very aware. As Emeril Lagasse would say, it "kicks it up a notch!"

- More excited and alive – With heightened senses and new experiences your adrenaline starts pumping. New things bring about excitement that makes you feel more alive. Where are new things found? Yep, outside your comfort zone!

- New experiences – You can't have a new experience if you remain in your comfort zone.

- Your comfort zone gets larger – Remember the first day you started school in let's say 5th grade? You were nervous and didn't really know what to expect. If only slightly, you were outside your comfort zone, but you had to stay in school. So what did you do? Probably just grinned and bore it. By the end of the year, however, walking into class wasn't hard to do because you knew exactly what to expect. Your comfort zone had expanded.

Dear friends, if you therefore want to live a life of riches, then you must learn to do what the rich do. You must be ready to put yourself in a temporary discomfort to have a permanent comfort. Nothing good comes easily they say. There is a price to pay for a life time of riches. One of those prices is stepping out of our comfort zone.

GOLDEN NUGGETS

1. Staying in our comfort zone is to live a life of discomfort

2. The ability to put ourselves in temporary discomfort to achieve our goals leads us to a life of permanent comfort.

3. The rich know how to put themselves in temporary discomfort to get a permanent comfort.

4. If you want to be rich, then do like the rich

5. There is no riches without taking risk

6. The greatest risk is risking nothing

7. The poor love comfort zones that is why they are poor

8. The rich have learnt to master their fear of moving out of their comfort zone

9. You must be ready to put yourself in a temporary discomfort in order to have a permanent comfort.

10. Everyone who ever did anything remarkable in history had to take a risk.

11. If you risk nothing you achieve nothing

12. You can only truly know yourself when you step out of your comfort zone.

CHAPTER 7

DEPENDENCY ON SALARY OR BEING A PAYCHECK LOVER

So many people today are tied to a paycheck. The system has so made it in such a way that, if you are not ready to take the bull by the horn, you can't live out of the grip of the paycheck syndrome. So many people are lost in life just working around the clock in order to make ends meet. Over 60% of the people in the world today do not like their jobs; they are only working because of the paycheck and nothing more. Over 70% of the world populations are in fields they don't have a natural flare for, just because of the high paycheck.

In Nigeria and Africa at large, it is almost like an abomination not to strive to get a paying job. Your value is being measured by the company or firm you work for. Living a life of dependence on salary is being celebrated. Almost all the young people graduating from the university are looking forward to getting a job and earning salary. That is their biggest dream. Sadly, that is the reason must people even go to school today. And this is not only in Africa, it is a global disease.

This however, is what the rich don't do that the poor do. The rich know that you cannot become rich by receiving paychecks while the poor are so tied to paychecks that they can't do without them. This is one of the major reasons why the rich get richer and the poor get poorer. The rich do not work for money; they put their money to work which means their money works for them while the poor work for money all their lives. As long as you continue to work for money you can never really become rich talk more of having financial freedom. Money is a good servant but a bad master. If you want to get a hold of money and a lot of it too, then you must learn to put it to work for you.

So many people even go to school, spend years studying, not necessarily what they were born to do but what gives them or makes them more marketable in the work place for a high paycheck. The irony of this whole process or drama is that, in most cases, this paycheck lovers are the ones that never get to financial freedom. The more increase in their paycheck the more their taxes increase, the more their wants increase. Hence they keep on running around the circle to make ends meet without getting to have a life of financial freedom. They become a permanent participant of the rate race.

> *To spend your life living in fear, never exploring your dreams is cruel. To work hard for money, thinking that it will buy you things that will make you happy is also cruel. To wake up in the middle of the night terrified about paying bills is a horrible way to live. To live a life dictated by the size of a paycheck is not really living a life. Thinking that a job makes you secure is lying to yourself. That's cruel, and that's a trap I want you to avoid (Robert T. Kiyosaki)*

You can never have financial freedom if you are totally dependent on paycheck. No one has ever attained financial freedom just by working for a paycheck. Am I saying it is wrong to work for a paycheck? No not at all, if that is what you want for your life, it is a matter of choice. But if you want to have financial freedom then you must not just depend on paychecks. Though you can work for a while for paychecks but that should be for a short while.

You must learn to invest and how to diversify your investments. You must be knowledgeable about the laws of money. You must know how money works. You have to be conversant with some monetary terms like asset, liability, inflation etc. unfortunately, it is this part that is absent in our school's curriculum. This very important part is what our schools don't teach. Therefore if you want to be financially free, you must step out of your comfort zone, to look for financial knowledge yourself or else you will become a prisoner to paycheck and salary.

I believe every one of us will like to be financially free, or more rightly put, dream of having financial freedom. But very few people have been able to obtain that. Why is that? It is because almost everybody works for money but very few know how money works. Those who become rich are not those that work for money but those that know how money works. I guess we are all familiar with the popular saying as I said earlier; money is a good slave but a bad master. Unfortunately not many of us have been able to put money to work for us or have the knowledge of how to do it. We have on more general scale made money our master. Since money is a bad master, that is why a lot of people end up being slaves to paycheck and living in penury from hand to mouth.

The SECRET to financial security is not to have more money, but having MORE CONTROL over the money we presently have. (Auliq-Ice)

It does not matter how many jobs you are working or how many paychecks you receive at the end of the month. If you do not know how money works, you will forever remain a slave to money, and will continue to work for paycheck. When it comes to the issue of financial freedom, it really does not depend on how hard you work. It is rather, how smart you can work and your level of knowledge about the principles of money and how to put money to work for you. When you have gained this understanding, then you are at the verge of your breakthrough. This is exactly what the rich know and practice that the poor do not know or if they know by chance do not practice.

The rich do not work for money, then put money to work for them. Working for money has not made anyone financially free. Do not be deceived, you are in no way different from others. If you continue to work for money, you will remain a slave to paycheck. So many people work for money because of the bills they have to pay. The system is wired in such a way that if you don't actually have this understanding you will think the only way out is to constantly work for a paycheck.

WHAT IS FINANCIAL FREEDOM

Financial freedom or independence is generally used to describe the state of having sufficient personal wealth to live without having to work actively for basic necessities. For financially independent people, their assets generate income that is greater than their expenses.

It is a point you get to that your needs do not have to decide what you do because you have all your needs met without actively working for money but your money is working for you. No one will ever get to this point in life by receiving paychecks alone. No matter the amount you receive in paychecks, it still will not give you financial freedom. This is a major truth the rich hold unto that the poor overlook or take for-granted.

> *Time, not money, is your biggest asset in life. You need time to invest in relationships (with yourself and your family) or to chase your passion. "Think again" if you are still trading off time for money. Let your money work for you. You don't work for money. That is exactly what Financial Freedom is... (Manoj Arora)*

How will you like to live and know that you don't have to work for life and still have all your needs met? It is the best kind of life one can live. Then you don't have to work for money but work in the area of your choice, doing what you love doing and fulfilling purpose. As we go deeper in this book I will be discussing with us how we can all achieve this in our lives. Please stay with me as we continue on our journey to financial freedom.

GOLDEN NUGGETS

1. Paycheck cannot give you financial freedom
2. Don't work for money but put your money to work for you.
3. You begin to live when your wants and needs do not decide what you do.
4. Living and knowing that you don't have to work for another man but will have all your needs met is the best kind of living.
5. Financial freedom is the greatest form of freedom.
6. The rich do not work for money, their money work for them.
7. The poor work for money and remain a prisoner to paycheck.
8. Money is a good servant but a bad master.
9. Having more money is not the key to financial freedom but how much control you have over the money you have.
10. Dependence on salary alone will only lead to poverty.
11. As long as you work for money you will remain a prisoner to the rat race.
12. Put your money to work and you will successfully move into financial freedom and independence.

CHAPTER 8
LIVING IN THE FEAR OF FAILURE AND MISTAKE

It is very important we know and understand that failure and mistake is a part of life. That is the first step to overcoming the fear of failure and mistake. The fear of failure had made more people poor and salary dependent than a bad economy.

People with abundance mindset have learnt to overcome and subdue their fear of failure and mistake. They have learnt to accept it as a part of life and an adventure that must be engaged in, in order to have a lasting success or financial freedom. The road to financial freedom is not void of risk. It is actually a risky part, but at the end of the day, it will land you into financial freedom.

If you don't want to ever fail or make any mistake in your life, then you are not ready to embark on any worthwhile venture. And as such you will remain a perpetual slave to your paycheck up until your retirement when you will have little or nothing to change the cause of events and opportunities you neglected and didn't take advantage of.

So many people are so afraid of how they are going to survive without a paycheck that they won't be able to pursue what they are passionate about. They don't want the temporal discomfort life will present them without a paycheck, or they are afraid, what if I quit my job and begin to pursue this business opportunity and I fail? What if I don't make it? What if I don't get another job?

"What if, what if, what if…?" have held so many people down than you can ever begin to imagine. I guess is high time you faced your fears, take the bull by the horn and set yourself free from financial slavery or slavery to paycheck.

The rich on the other hand have learnt to master their fear of mistake and failure. They know that life itself is a risk and for you to make anything worthwhile out of life you must be willing and apt to take risk. You must be ready to take a leap of faith with your eyes closed. You must be prepared to live and embrace temporal discomfort if that is what it will take for you to get to your desired financial destination. This is the lifestyle of the rich that the poor are yet to know, learn or master.

Before you undertake any venture though, you must get or acquire all the knowledge necessary for the journey you are embarking on. Never step out into any business venture you do not have a thorough knowledge or understanding about. The more knowledge you have about an area you want to venture into the less risk you will have. Knowledge reduces the risk by over 50 percent. That is a big reduction I guess, so you don't want to take the issue of knowledge lightly if you must succeed in a business venture.

Surround yourself with those who are knowledgeable in your area of interest. Learn from the best and you become the best. Take advice from only those who have results to show for their advice. No one can ever give what they don't have.

It's better to hang out with people better than you. Pick out associates whose behaviour is better than yours and you'll drift in that direction. (Warren Buffett)

If you want to go into shoe business, don't go to a school teacher or banker to take advice. Don't just even take advice from any shoe dealer. Rather look for the successful ones in the business and seek for advice from them. Learn from them what they did to be successful in that business. The more knowledge you have the fewer mistakes you will make and the higher your chances of success in that endeavour. In order to overcome your fears, load yourself with the necessary knowledge required.

What are the things you are afraid of? What exactly is your biggest fear? What do you think is the worst that can happen? For you to have your desired financial freedom, you must learn to face your fears. Well you might want to ask me, how do I overcome my fears? I really want to but I don't know how. This is how:

First, face your financial fears. Take some time and make a list of what is causing you to be anxious and fearful. Is it the economy, your job stability, investment account balances, your children's education funds, or the amount of debt you are carrying? Try to be specific and detailed in your concerns. Now study that list very carefully — is there anything on that list that you can do something about?

Second, take action. Create a budget that paints a clear picture of your income and expenses. Remember that the basic rules of personal financial planning remain the same regardless of the economic environment.

Whether the economy is good or bad, you should live within your means, save the difference in an emergency fund for investment opportunity, and pay down debt. If your house payments are overwhelming, then start the process of refinancing. If you are making just the minimum payments on your credit cards, call the company and work out a payment schedule that is feasible. Continually develop your skills set and be on the lookout for investment opportunities.

Fear is the elephant in the room that will destroy the furnishings if ignored. Fear and inertia cause people to make irrational choices. By seeking out accurate information and relevant knowledge, on the other hand, you can take actions that will reduce your financial fears and put you in control.

Third, invest in planning. Part of moving on financially is coming up with a written financial plan. This serves as a compass when we become excessively exuberant or overly pessimistic. The plan should address not only your short-term financial goals but also your long-term objectives. It should detail a personal income statement and balance sheet. This presents an objective picture of where you are. The next step is determining where you want to go — financially speaking — and outlining the steps to get there.

By working with a financial advisor, you can gain an objective perspective on your financial "big picture." Having a financial quarterback, someone with an educated and independent outlook, is worth its weight in gold. An advisor can help you work to enhance your financial plan via money management. Depending on their credentials, they may recommend specific investments, long-term investing strategies, insurance options, retirement planning, risk management methods, and more.

Sit down with the advisor and ask about their credentials, how they operate, and their years of experience. Be sure it is someone you feel comfortable with and that your personalities mesh. The right financial planner will help you determine both your short-term and long-term goals and help you develop an action plan to meet those goals. You can visit the Certified Financial Planners website to find a financial advisor with proven credentials in your area, or one who has a particular expertise.

Another big misconception people have is that they think for you to really achieve financial freedom, you have to have a lot of money to invest in the first place but that's not necessarily the case. Ordinary people with ordinary jobs and savings accounts can put themselves on the path to financial freedom just by making sure that they add to their savings account regularly and make safe investments and live frugally, saving money where they can.

You really don't need to start big to achieve financial freedom. You can start where you are. Get rid of your fears or better still do it afraid. Take your financial destiny into your hands and stop waiting for anyone to do it for. Don't wait for the government, you might wait for all your life and be disappointed. Don't wait for the economy to get better; you might have to wait for eternity. You have to take charge of your financial life. If other people can be financially free in the same economy, there is no reason why that person shouldn't be you.

Do not let the fear of failure hold you back. Every successful person we celebrate today, have had their own share of failure. But they did not allow failure or the fear of failing hold them back. They forged ahead through the failure and moved into their life time of success and financial freedom. Did you know that...?

Bill Gates watched his first company crumble

Bill Gates is now one of the world's wealthiest individuals, but he didn't earn his fortune in a straight line to success. Gates entered the entrepreneurial scene with a company called Traf-O-Data, which aimed to process and analyze the data from traffic tapes (think of it like an early version of big data).

He tried to sell the idea alongside his business partner, Paul Allen, but the product barely even worked. It was a complete disaster. However, the failure did not hold Gates back from exploring new opportunities, and a few years later, he created his first Microsoft product, and forged a new path to success.

Walt Disney was told he lacked creativity

One of the most creative geniuses of the 20th century was once fired from a newspaper outfit because he was told he lacked creativity. Trying to persevere, Disney formed his first animation company, which was called Laugh-O-Gram Films. He raised $15,000 for the company but eventually was forced to close Laugh-O-Gram, following the close of an important distributor partner.

Desperate and out of money, Disney found his way to Hollywood and faced even more criticism and failure until finally, his first few classic films started to skyrocket in popularity.

Milton Hershey started three candy companies before Hershey's

Everyone knows Hershey's chocolate, but when Milton Hershey first started his candy production career, he was a nobody. After being fired from an apprenticeship with a printer, Hershey started three separate candy-related ventures, and was forced to watch all of them fail. In one last attempt, Hershey founded the Lancaster Caramel Company, and started seeing enormous results. Believing in his vision for milk chocolate for the masses, he eventually founded the Hershey Company and became one of the most well-known names in the industry.

Draw inspiration from these stories and let it kill your fear of failure. Accept failure as a part of your journey to success and freedom. Don't allow yourself to be gripped by the fear of failure. If you fail know that that is not the end of the road. Your failure should be a reminder to you that success is ahead of you if only you don't give up. The next time you experience failure, no matter the scale, get up and keep going don't stop until you reach your destination called success. In the moment, some failure might seem like the end of the road, but remember, there are countless successful men and women in the world today who are only enjoying success because they decided to push past the inevitable bleakness of failure. Learn from your mistakes, reflect and accept the failure, but revisit your passion and keep pursuing your goals no matter what.

You too can succeed even after failure. So banish the fear of failure and move on to embrace your success and financial freedom waiting for you on the other side.

GOLDEN NUGGETS

. . . .

1. Failure and mistakes are a part of life.

2. Every successful person has had his own share of failure.

3. Learn from your failure and move on

4. The rich have mastered their fear of failure

5. The poor allow their fear of failure hold them back.

6. You can succeed after failure.

7. That you failed is not the end. Get up and keep moving.

8. Face your fears and take the bull by the horn.

9. If you don't want to ever fail or make any mistake in your life, then you are not ready to embark on any worthwhile venture.

10. You really don't need to start big to achieve financial freedom

11. Surround yourself with those who are knowledgeable in your area of interest.

12. Never step out into any business venture you do not have a thorough knowledge or understanding about.

CHAPTER 9
INABILITY TO DELAY GRATIFICATION

The primary reason for financial problems in most people's lives is lack of self-discipline, self-mastery, and self-control. It is the inability to delay gratification in the short term. It is the tendency for people to spend everything they earn and a little more besides, usually supplemented by loans and credit card debt.

We are living in the most beautiful time in all of human history. There are more opportunities to achieve wealth and prosperity today, for more people, in various ways than have ever existed in the history of man. It has never been more possible for you to achieve financial independence than right now. But you must make a resolution to do it, and then follow through on your resolution.

Financial Problems

The primary reason for financial problems is not necessarily caused by low earnings. The number one reason is lack of self-discipline and the inability to delay gratification. Why is this weakness of character so prevalent among the majority of adults in the society today? It goes back to early childhood.

When you were a child and you received money (whether it was your allowance or a gift from a friend or relative), the first thing you thought of doing was to spend that money on candy. Candy is sweet. Candy is delicious. Candy fills your mouth with a wonderful, sugary flavor. You liked candy when you were a child, and you probably could seldom get enough of it. Many children will eat candy until they become physically ill because it tastes so good.

As you grew older, you developed what psychologists call a "conditioned response" to receiving money from any source. Like Pavlov's dog, when you receive money, you mentally salivate at the thought of spending this money on something that makes you happy, at least temporarily.

SPENDING MONEY MAKES YOU HAPPY

When you become an adult and you earn or receive money, this automatic reaction continues. Your first thought is, "How can I spend this money to achieve immediate pleasure?"

Have you noticed that when you go on vacation to a resort of any kind, you find that the hotels and streets are lined with shops selling useless trinkets, bobbles and trash, plus clothes, artwork, and other items that you would never think of buying at home? Why is this? Simple, when you are on vacation, you feel happy. You have a conditioned response to associate happiness with spending money. The happier you are, the more unconsciously compelled you are to go out and spend money on something, or on anything.

It is quite common for many people, when they are unhappy or frustrated for any reason, to go shopping. They unconsciously associate buying something with being happy. When it doesn't work as they expected, they buy something else. Sometimes, unhappy people go on shopping sprees. They buy lots of things that they don't particularly need because they unconsciously associate spending with happiness.

USE SELF DISCIPLINE TO ACHIEVE DELAYED GRATIFICATION

The starting point of achieving financial independence is for you to use self-discipline to reorder your attitude towards money. You reach into your subconscious mind and disconnect the wire linking "spending" and "happiness." You then reconnect that "happiness" wire to the "saving and investing" wire. This is what the rich do that makes them rich and the poor don't do. The rich understands the power of delayed gratification and they practice and put this power to work and the result is always more wealth.

To reinforce this shift in thinking and eliminate financial problems, open up a "financial freedom account" at your local bank. This is the account in which you deposit money for the long term. Once your money goes into this account, you resolve that you will never spend it on anything except for investment which will lead to achieving financial freedom.

ASSOCIATE HAPPINESS WITH FINANCIAL FREEDOM

When you begin saving in this way, something miraculous happens within you. You start to feel happy about the idea of having money in the bank. Even if you only open your account with $10, this action gives you a feeling of greater self-control and personal power. You feel happier about yourself.

Because the money in your account is emotionalized by your own thoughts and feelings, it sets up a force field of energy that begins to attract more money into it. If you save $10 a month for a year, you will be astonished to find that with the extra bits of money that you have put into that account, you will probably have more than $200, rather than just $120. If you save $100 per month, you will probably have more than $2,000.

The more money you have in your bank account, the more energy it generates and the more money is attracted into your life. You have heard it said that, "It takes money to make money." This is true. As you begin to save and accumulate money, the universe begins to direct more and more money towards you, to save and accumulate and invest. Everyone who has ever practiced this principle of regular saving is absolutely astonished at how quickly their financial problems change for the better.

The rule for financial independence, once you have reordered your attitude toward money, is to "Pay yourself first." Most people save whatever is left over after their monthly expenses, if there is anything left over. The key however is to pay yourself first, off the top, of every amount of money you receive.

This reminds me of the story of a traveler in the desert who was almost dying of thirst when he stumbled upon an abandoned cabin with a manual pump at the backyard. Beside the well was a bottle of water with a note on a piece of paper attached. Curious, he opened the note to read. It was instructions on how to prime the pump. He was to pour the water in the bottle down a hole beside the pump and start pumping the handle to prime the pump.

He had a tough decision to make – drink the water in the bottle (which had gotten quite warm) or pour it down a hole and prime the pump for water to come out of the well. He realized the bottle of warm water, though may not refresh as much will at least quench his thirst to a large extent. But after drinking the bottle of water, what next? Pouring it down a hole was a risk. What if his attempt to prime the pump fails? He will be back to square one, as thirsty as hell. But again, that is where he will eventually end up long after drinking the water in the bottle anyway.

He decided to take the risk. He poured the water down the hole and started pumping the handle of the pump. For some scary minutes, nothing happened. After a while, he heard a sound. Water started gushing out. Clean cool and fresh water. He drank to his fill, filled up his containers, took a cool bath, stayed in the cabin for a while as he plotted his way back to civilization. He delayed gratification.

For most of us, we would have drunk down the bottle of warm water and hope for the best. We would be living from hand to mouth, praying for the next bottle of water, no matter how dirty. Our focus would shift from finding our way home to searching for the next drink. We would end up going round in circles, looking for water rather than finding our way home. Sadly, that is the case with most salary earners.

Until we let go the bottle of water and prime the pump, we will keep working for money rather than creating assets (accessing the well for water) that will work

85

hard for us. It simply takes ignoring our thirsts for a few moments to allow the water from the well come through.

Paul and Richard are brothers born to same parents. After their father's death his properties were divided between the two brothers. Paul who was the oldest took his own share of the property and went on spending. Buying choice cars, gadgets and other lovely things of life that can meet the eye. Richard on the other hand delayed gratification and went into investing his share of his father's properties that was given to him. Ten years down the line Paul went bankrupt but Richard is living in wealth, he has succeeded in tripling what was left for him from his father's earnings and properties. Delayed gratification always pays at the end of the day.

"No matter how great the talent or efforts, some things just take time. You can't produce a baby in one month by getting nine women pregnant." (Warren Buffet)

If your desire is to obtain riches and live in financial freedom, then you have to learn and practice what the rich do. They delay gratification in order to invest for a permanent gratification.

GOLDEN NUGGETS

1. Learn to delay temporal gratification and invest in order to have permanent gratification.
2. Don't connect happiness with spending
3. Connect happiness with saving
4. Pay yourself first.
5. It takes money to make money. Money at hand has a way of attracting more money to you.
6. One major reason for financial lack is the lack of self-discipline and the inability to delay gratification.
7. Change your attitude towards money.
8. It takes discipline to delay gratification.
9. Associate happiness will financial freedom
10. There is confidence that comes in having money in the bank that attracts money to you.
11. Don't go on a spending spree just to be happy.
12. Let your happiness come from the size of your account and investment.

CHAPTER 10

THE DESIRE TO PLEASE EVERYONE WITHOUT SETTING PERSONAL PRIORITIES

Everyone loves to be loved by others! We often go to great lengths to please people so they will like or love us. This is a natural desire since God has made us all social beings. This drive to be accepted can help build our self-esteem. Yet, this same desire can also become unhealthy when the desire to please is so great that one ignores sound principles in order to find acceptance by others.

If there is anything you must know and understand it is that money is not emotional. You need to take emotions out of your financial life if you must succeed. What do I mean by this?

You have to know that people will always have needs. They will always have one thing or the other they want you to do, help them or a need they want you to meet, especially family members and friends. You have to learn to plan and have a financial budget that you never exceed no matter what. This is where you have to control your emotions. People will come to you with all kinds of needs and wants that if you do not have your plan in place, you will give your all and start begging yourself.

I use to be like that myself. Because I am very sympathetic to the needs of people and any challenges whatsoever they have, due to the fact that I love people. But one

89

thing you should understand is that giving alone does not make anyone rich; neither does it lead to financial freedom. Am I in any way saying you shouldn't give? No not at all. I am a giver myself. What I am saying rather is that you should give with wisdom and discretion.

Our life is the sum total of all the decisions we make every day, and those decisions are determined by our priorities. (Myles Munroe)

You have to set your priorities straight. Make a laid down principle and make sure you follow it to the letter. How do you do this? You need to make your financial plan in this way, for instance:

1. I have to remove 10% of my income for my tithe
2. I have to pay myself. Maybe 10%, 20%, 30% or even more depending on your financial capacity.
3. The money I pay myself is not for spending but for saving and investment.
4. Take out another 10% for charity.
5. 50% of my income for my upkeep and bills.
6. Make sure your monthly expenses stays with 50-70% of your income. Never spend anything more than 70%

For everyone that will be coming to ask you for financial assistance or one need or the other, the money you need to take from is the 10% you kept aside for charity. The moment you have exhausted that budget you have for helping others, don't go any further. Every other need or assistance they ask of you should wait till the next month.

Don't make the mistake of going to take money from the money you paid yourself to help anyone. Know that the moment you have kept that money aside it is no longer yours. So it will be ok to tell them that you do not have any other money, they should wait till next month. For you to be able to do this, you have to learn to keep your emotions aside and follow your priorities if you want to be rich. If not you will continue to live from paycheck to paycheck, from hand to mouth. Before your check gets into your hand you have already spent it.

It is OK for people not to be happy with you for a while, than for you to live in financial slavery all your life. When you finally have your financial freedom, you will be able to give and help them more even on a large scale. But now that you are building, you need to build with wisdom and learn to be very frugal with your expenses and spending. Don't put others above yourself. Set your personal priorities straight and follow it whole heartedly.

Don't lend your money to anyone. You are not a bank. If they want to borrow money let them go to the bank and borrow. The fastest way to losing your friends or turning friends to enemies is by lending them money. I will rather advice you give them what you can afford to lose or let go and let them go somewhere else to complete the money. Or better still give them as a gift, what you can afford. Don't let your emotions drive you to accepting a pity party story or you will live to regret it.

Never allow people push you into not respecting or keeping to your priorities. You will need discipline and will-power to turn deaf ears to anything or expenses that is not in your budget. A budget well followed is a sure path to financial freedom and independence. Stay in charge of your financial life, and be an effective manager of your resources or otherwise, a life of penury and frustration that comes with debt and poverty will be your company. I know that is not the kind of life you want for yourself, therefore your financial freedom should be paramount.

GOLDEN NUGGETS

1. You don't need to please everyone at your own expense.
2. Follow through with your financial plan no matter what.
3. Don't lend your money to anyone, you are not a bank
4. Lending money to friends is the easiest way of turning friends into enemies.
5. While building, never place people's needs above your financial plan.
6. Giving alone will not make you rich.
7. Money is not emotional.
8. Take emotions away from money.
9. If you give to every need that presents itself, you will soon join the begging team.
10. Don't give or spend the money you paid yourself.
11. Know that the money you pay yourself is for investment and not yours to spend.
12. It is ok for people not to be happy with you for a while, than for you to live in financial slavery all your life.

CHAPTER 11

SCHOOL EDUCATION IS KEY TO FINANCIAL FREEDOM

Most of us have had the advice from our parents or well-wishers to study hard, go to college, get a degree so you can get a good job and have financial freedom. What a myth this advice is today! Maybe it worked 20-50 years back, but in our present generation, just school education is not enough, it is not a guarantee to financial freedom. School education is no key to financial freedom. If it was the key, then those with great degrees, multiple degrees, and educational scholars should be the richest. In the real sense of it, the reverse is the case.

It is high time we faced the reality before us, and grasp our financial destiny into our hands by going out to seek for information by ourselves. The wisdom for financial freedom is not taught in schools unfortunately. No school teaches you the laws of money, no degree in colleges teaches how to live and have financial freedom. Our educational sectors only prepare you to be a job seeker, a paycheck lover, and finally a financial slave to the system.

Well, no one will tell you this in the real sense of it but this is what is obtainable in our present day corrupt system. Where the wealth of the world is being controlled by the few 2% while the remaining 98% live from paycheck to paycheck, hand to mouth. Let me make this clear to you, this 2% of the world population who live in financial freedom, did not steal from others to be in this position because we like making excuses for reasons why we can't have financial freedom. They are rather where they are because of what they know. It is therefore my earnest desire for you to seek to know what they know that has placed them in the position where they are today.

That is the reason for this book. To bring you the financial education, principles and laws of money that the wealthy 2% of the world live by. So if you want to move from the 98% of those in lack to the wealthy 2% of the world, then continue reading this book, but if not you can as well discontinue reading this book now, because this book will not in any way teach how to chase or seek for jobs. It will rather set you free from being dependent on jobs.

As much as I am a big fan of school education, as much as I encourage you to get a degree, I will not hesitate to let you know, that this alone will not give you financial freedom. So as you are pursuing your college degree, also pursue financial education. Get knowledge on how to make money work for you. You can only know this when you know the laws of money.

The rich do not work for money; they put their money to work for them. You cannot be wealthy if you continue to work for money without putting money to work for you. Those who make money their servants or slaves become wealthy, because money is a good servant but a bad master. When you master the laws of money, then you will learn how to send your money to work and make more money for you. Your money can work tirelessly for you than you can ever work for yourself. Your money will work for you 24 hours a day, seven days a week, when the average person who works for money, only works 8-10 hours daily, 4-5 days a week.

Now it is obvious why those who put their money to work get wealthy and those who work for money don't. It is rather unfortunate that the only thing the school system teaches us is how to work for money. That is why we have so much brilliant and intelligent minds today in our society that are broke. They are carrying so many degrees with empty pockets barely making ends meet.

The universe is not limited in its resources to humanity. Humanity is rather limited in their minds. They are limited in how to put their mind to work and get the universe to release for them what is rightfully theirs. We don't always get what we deserve, we get what we demand. Until you have learnt to lay hold on the knowledge of wealth creation and demand of the universe what is rightfully yours by applying the laws of money and the principle of wealth creation, you will die in poverty with all the potential of financial freedom, lying dormant within you.

Wake up from this great deception that has led many in the direction of financial slavery and embrace the reality of financial freedom by getting financial education, which of course you will get from this book. I will be dealing in details on this in our subsequent chapters. It is about time you said fare-well to a life of dependence on paycheck. It is high time you set yourself free from the shackles of working so hard trying to make ends meet, which never gets to meet at the end of the day.

We have three basic kinds of education today, out of these three only one has what it takes to give you financial freedom. But it is this particular one that is not being thought in our schools. They are: academic education, professional education and financial education.

Academic Education:

This is what we all have gone to school to learn. It is very important and teaches us the foundation of how to read, write, learn and function in the world.

Professional Education:

This is what we learn to help us to be successful in our careers. We may learn this in college or trade school or the job. It is the information and skills we need to be successful at our work.

Financial Education:

This is the type of education that teaches us what we should be doing with our money to be successful. In today's world, financial education is crucial, especially with the world economy in recession or depression. However, our school systems do not teach us about financial education and so most people have never been taught what they need to know in order to take control of their financial lives.

It is therefore our responsibility to step out to seek that knowledge, which is what you are doing now by reading this book. Stay with me and soon you will get to discover that living a life of financial freedom is not a mystery nor is it unobtainable. I am not saying it is easy but it is simple and doable.

To bring this point home, and give you a clear picture of what this chapter is about, I will like us to end this chapter by looking at some examples of people who made it to financial freedom without college degrees. Remember, I am not saying academic or professional education is not important. The point here is, when it comes to financial freedom, college degree is not the key.

1. Sir Richard Branson. Founder of the Virgin
   Group

Richard Branson not only didn't attend college; he was a high school dropout. A born entrepreneur, he launched his first business, Student magazine, at the age of 16. At 19, he started a mail-order record shop called Virgin. Its success led Branson to launch the recording studio, Virgin Records. In 1980, Branson added travel businesses to his holdings, including Voyager Group and Virgin Atlantic airlines. In 1999, Branson was knighted by Prince Charles of Wales to honor his contribution to entrepreneurship. Today, Virgin Group has more than 200 companies in 30 countries.

2. Michael Dell. Founder of Dell Computers

A former pre-med student, Michael Dell dropped out of the University of Texas during his sophomore year to found Dell Computers. He formed an interest in computers in the early 1980s when the personal computer industry was still in its infancy. Building and selling PCs directly to customers, he dropped out of school to focus on his business. During its first year, Dell Computers had $6 million in sales. In 1992, Dell was named the youngest CEO on the Fortune 500 list of the top corporations. Today, Dell Computers is one of the world's largest PC makers.

3. Evan Williams. Co-founder and former CEO
   of Twitter

Evan Williams attended the University of Nebraska for a year and a half before leaving school to pursue a freelance career in information systems. He did work for Hewlett-Packard and Intel before he and partner

Meg Hourihan launched the blogging platform Blogger, which was acquired by Google in 2003. He and Noah Glass founded the podcast company Odeo where he hired Biz Stone and Jack Dorsey. The four men—none of whom hold college degrees—eventually brainstormed the micro-blogging platform Twitter in 2006. The company went public in November 2013.

4. Jan Koum. Co-founder and CEO of the mobile messaging service WhatsApp

Jan Koum grew up in a rural area outside Kiev, Ukraine, and immigrated to California with his mother when he was 16. Koum dropped out of San Jose State University, where he was studying math and computer science, and took a job at Yahoo where he worked for nine years in systems security and infrastructure engineering. He got the idea for WhatsApp in 2009 as a way to display status messages next to friends in your address book. It eventually became a mobile messaging system with 450 million monthly users. In February 2014, Facebook acquired WhatsApp for a reported $19 billion.

GOLDEN NUGGETS

• • • • • • • • • • • • •

1. School education is not a guarantee to financial freedom

2. A degree is not a ticket to financial freedom.

3. It is possible to be educated and yet be an illiterate financially.

4. Financial education is absent in our schools, therefore self-education is the answer.

5. The old advice, go to college in order to make a living is a myth today.

6. Embrace the reality of financial freedom by getting financial education. The knowledge that liberates.

7. Your financial destiny is a personal responsibility.

8. Living a financially free life is not a mystery

9. Financial freedom can be attained by everyone. It might not be easy but is simple and doable.

10. There are three types of education: Academic education, professional education and financial education.

11. The type of education you have is the distance between you and your financial freedom.

12. All three educations are very important. But when it comes to financial freedom, financial education is the key.

CHAPTER 12

FINANCIAL DEGREE EQUALS FINANCIAL ABUNDANCE

Financial degree is not in any way equivalent to financial freedom or abundance. Well, as much as we would have thought that those who go to school to get a professional degree in finance will know more about money, the laws of money, principles of money, and how to make money to work in order to live in financial freedom, the reverse is the case.

Just as I mentioned earlier above, that financial education is not taught in our schools or colleges is no joke. All that is taught in our schools is how to work for money. They train you to be your best, so you will be marketable in the market place. When they say marketable, do you bother to ask what exactly they mean by this? Well, it simply means, training you to be more qualified as an employee, working for and dependent on paychecks. That is not necessarily bad if that is what you want. But if what you need is financial freedom, then that is in no way getting you there.

This is the discovery that those with abundance mindset have. The one thing that the rich do not do but the poor do. The rich do not go to school to pursue a degree in order to get a job. As much as degree is of essence, they don't put their hope in getting a degree to lead them to financial freedom. They rather go out of their way to seek financial knowledge and educate themselves financially. They do not leave their financial fate in the hands

103

of our educational system. They take the bull by the horn and source for the knowledge needed in other to be financially free.

There are so many people who are living in financial abundance and freedom today that never went to college. There are so many graduates, master's degree holders, PhD holders who are working and living from hands to mouth trying to make ends meet. So you will agree with me that financial degree is not equivalent to financial freedom. Financial knowledge is what leads to financial freedom not financial degree.

Mr. Joe was a man of little modern day education; he never went to college but was privileged to be exposed to books. He embarked on self-educating himself. Going to the library to study was one of his hobbies. On this faithful day, on his way from the library, he met one of the richest men in his city. He greeted him, and asked the man if he had 5 minutes to spare, to which the rich man obliged him.

Mr. Joe asked the rich man, what can I do to be rich? Can you teach me what it takes to be rich? The rich man looked at him, and smiled. He said to him, young man, I like your courage and boldness. I will teach you how to be rich, but on the condition that you will serve me for five years. To this Mr. Joe agreed immediately without wasting time. That was how his journey to financial freedom started.

He served him for five years, during this period of serving him, the rich man taught Mr. Joe all he needed to be rich. He taught him the laws and principles of money, how to put money to work for you, saving and investments. After the five years of serving the rich man, Mr. Joe was ready to face the world to seek for financial freedom. On the day of his departure, the rich man gave Mr. Joe some money to start up himself in life. This money became Joe's capital force to financial freedom.

Just two years afterwards, Joe has already flourished in his business, and began to expand. By the third year, he started his first company. Even though he had little modern day education, he became an employer of labor to graduates of colleges and master's degree holders. He employed the best of the best to work for him and formed his mastermind alliance. It was not long afterwards, his company grew so fast and Mr. Joe began to float in financial abundance. Even though he didn't have any college education, today he is living in financial freedom. He has provided several job opportunities to so many people in his society.

So you see, financial degree is not in any way equal to financial abundance, freedom or knowledge.

One question on the minds of college students everywhere is this: What degree is going to provide me with the very best opportunity to become truly successful? And this same question is often very much on the minds of people already working full time who want to get a second degree - perhaps an MBA or other graduate degree - to boost their work skills and career prospects.

U.K.-based Approved Index took a close look at Forbes's list of the 100 wealthiest people in the world to answer this question, and the results are often surprising. Consider these facts:

32 percent of billionaires do not have a college degree. (Famously, Bill Gates, Oprah Winfrey, Steve Jobs,

and Mark Zuckerberg all dropped out of college prior to completing a degree, and the dyslexic Richard Branson dropped out of high school.)

Twice as many billionaires have degrees in the arts as in math and science. The average age of the billionaires in Approved Index's survey is 68. So, what college degree will make you rich? Perhaps no college degree at all. Here's the breakdown for the world's 100 wealthiest people, according to Approved Index:

32% No college degree
22% Engineering
12% Business
10% Other
9% Arts
8% Economics
3% Finance
2% Science
2% Mathematics

"These findings undoubtedly add a new dimension to the debate about the relevance and value of a degree today, and certainly suggest that in order to have a thriving and diverse economy, we need to encourage a varied range of specializations," says Amy Catlow, a director at Approved Index.

I will like you to have this at the back of your mind. It does not matter what degree you have or what you studied, as long as you are living from paycheck to paycheck, that is you are working for someone as your only source of income. You can never have financial freedom.

GOLDEN NUGGETS

1. No degree will give you financial freedom as long as you work for paychecks.
2. A financial degree does not equal financial freedom
3. Financial freedom is obtainable without a degree
4. 32% of billionaires do not have college degree
5. You can have a financial degree and not know the laws of money.
6. The only key to financial freedom is financial knowledge applied
7. The rich do not get a degree in hope to get financial freedom
8. The poor pursue degree in hope to get financial freedom
9. Ours schools train you to work for money
10. The poor get college degree to be marketable as an employee.
11. The rich get college degree as a tool to enhance their capacity.
12. If your goal is financial freedom, then chase financial knowledge not degree.

CHAPTER 13

THE BELIEF IN LUCK AND CHANCE AS KEY TO FINANCIAL FREEDOM

As unbelievable as this may sound, so many people still believe that financial freedom is a result of luck or chance. I have talked to so many people who approached me complaining of their financial ordeals in life, telling me that they don't know why they are so unlucky. The religious ones will say that they don't know why God has not brought luck their way. Others believe they have tried everything humanly possible and riches are not forth coming. As such everyone was not meant to be rich but the few that are lucky by fate. According to them when fate smiles on you then riches will find you or you become rich.

The people with the poverty mindset are of the school of thought that riches come by chance. I think all these thoughts are the highest form of delusion. On the other hand, those with the abundance mindset know that there is no such thing as getting rich by chance or luck. As a matter of fact everyone has luck but those who become lucky are those who are prepared, who have developed themselves to take advantage of luck when the opportunity shows up. Opportunity they say will always meet the prepared.

Thomas Jefferson rightly said it

"I'm a greater believer in luck, and I find the harder I work the more I have of it"

Before you complain of how unlucky you are, I will like you to answer this simple question. How prepared are you? How well can you take advantage of luck when it comes your way? Will you even notice it when it comes? It takes a developed mind to see luck when it comes and to take advantage of it. Luck comes in forms of opportunities, but sadly many people do not even recognize an opportunity when it shows up. It passes them by because they are not prepared. Only those who are well prepared make good use of their opportunities. They are the ones we call lucky.

Wake up my friend, these people are not just lucky, they have paid the price of personal development and preparations. You also can get lucky by going through the process they went through and doing what they did. They did not just wake up one morning to see their sitting room filled with money; neither did they just discover money growing on the trees in their garden. They worked for it. There is no such thing as just being lucky without working. You can't get something for nothing.

It is high time we quit believing that we are not lucky that is why we are not rich. Know that riches do not come by chance. Nothing in life happens by chance. Life is based on principles. Just as financial freedom or abundance is based on principles. Anyone who applies these principles will have the same results. The space might be different, the capacity, speed and quantity might be different. Because it is all based on how much of these principles you know, and how much discipline you have been able to put in place to make sure it comes to fruition in your life.

Financial freedom only comes by applying financial laws and living by the principles of money. If these two things are at work in your life, you have no need worrying about lack, because that will soon be history. Even though it will not happen in a day or automatically, it does take time. But one thing is certain, it will surely happen.

THE GOOSE THAT LAY THE GOLDEN EGG

You remember the old story about a farmer that discovered his goose was laying golden eggs. But then he got greedy and decided to kill the goose to get all the eggs out at once only to discover that there was nothing inside and he had killed off his chance of getting any more golden eggs? Well this is a good analogy we can use for investing, in that we can build up a goose (or lump sum) that will then pay us our golden eggs (or ongoing income).

To be financially free, we must first build our asset base or lump sum that is going to pay us our ongoing income. So the very first thing we need to do is open up a separate account and start to deposit 10 percent of our income into this account. The best way to do this is to open up a high interest online banking account and set up an automatic deduction as soon as you get paid. It works with the principle of paying yourself first, and when it is done automatically as soon as you get paid you will never miss the money! This account will then become your Financial Freedom account or FFA account.

If you are not used to this principle, start first with a lower percentage and build up the amount over time.

But make sure you start because without this account and building up your goose, you will NEVER be financially free! Your FFA account will serve as your preparation that will get you ready to take advantage of luck (opportunity) when it comes your way. With the money you have saved (lump sum) you can take advantage of business opportunities and invest in them. This is how to be lucky.

So once this lump sum starts to build up, you can start investing for your golden eggs. Start to invest in a variety of assets that will give you both cash flow and growth. Over time this asset base will build up and eventually it will start to pay you in ongoing residual or passive income in the form of dividends, interest, equity or residual income from your business. But remember the principle must be NEVER EVER SPENT! Don't be like the farmer and kill the goose!

So in summary unless we can build our asset base and create ongoing residual income, or in other words our goose that lays our golden eggs, we can never be financially free. So the key is to open our financial freedom account, pay ourselves first and create our goose that will lay our golden eggs. Luck alone cannot make you rich!

GOLDEN NUGGETS

1. Luck will not make you rich
2. Everyone has luck but only the prepared becomes lucky.
3. It takes hard work to be able to take advantage of luck.
4. There is no such thing as just being lucky financially without work
5. Riches do not come by chance
6. Those we call lucky are those who have paid the price of personal development.
7. Riches are not a function of fate.
8. Everyone can be lucky through hard work
9. No one is destined to be poor
10. We become poor or rich by what we know or don't know.
11. Those with the abundance mindset know that it takes work to create a fortune not luck.
12. The way to have more luck is the way of hard work.

CHAPTER 14

THE BELIEVE THAT PRAYER MAKES ONE RICH

I will like to start this chapter by saying that I do believe in prayers. I love to pray and I pray a lot too. Having said that, I will like you to understand that prayer does not put money in anyone's pocket. As a matter of fact, the richest people in our world today are not those who are very much skilled in prayer, but those who have learnt the principles of money and are applying them. It is of no use to believe that prayer is the key to your financial freedom.

Many religious people today are poor because of this deception they have believed in. Instead of stepping out to work and get knowledge on how to be financially free, they lock up themselves in buildings, praying and calling on God to come and do for them what they are supposed to do for themselves. Permit me to say that this is the highest form of laziness, indolence, negligence and laxity.

God has already placed on the earth, all you need to be successful. There is nothing you need that is not already available on the earth. So why are you wasting your time calling on God to come give you what you already have been given on the earth. That is like praying that God should come and get you water to drink, when you have a glass of water right in front of you staring at you. This is however what we do when we go to pray for financial freedom, instead of getting to work and seeking for financial laws and principles. Don't stop at seeking it, when you find it, begin to apply it in your everyday life in order to reap the harvest that is abounding everywhere on the earth.

Money does not go to those who need money. Money goes to those who know how to put money to work. Those who can command money rightly are the ones money goes to. Stop praying and get to work. Money will not rain down from heaven to you. The earth has surplus untapped resources that can go around in surplus to humanity at large. The problem is not with lack of resources. The problem is the lack of knowledge, knowledge on how money works, and knowledge of how to make financial freedom a reality in our everyday life.

Isn't it high time, we put our brains to work? For how long will you keep on doing the same thing over and over again even when you are not getting any tangible result? Why not just sit back and do a quick analysis? How many rich people in the world today got rich because of how wonderfully well they could pray? How many people living in financial freedom have that because they are the best prayer warriors the world has ever known? I bet you already know what the answers to these questions are. Tell yourself the truth today and set out on a right path towards your financial freedom. Get to work, most of all, put the financial knowledge and principles you are reading in this book to work and watch the transformation take place in your life.

GOLDEN NUGGETS

1. Prayer alone will not make you rich
2. Prayer warriors are not the richest on earth
3. Prayer does not give financial freedom
4. Prayer will not replace financial knowledge
5. Prayer is not the key to riches
6. Stop praying for riches and start working
7. Money does not go to those who need money
8. Money goes to those who can put money to work
9. Money will not rain down from heaven to you
10. There are enough resources on the earth for all.
11. The problem is not lack of resources.
12. The problem is lack of knowledge.

CHAPTER 15

BEING GOOD AND GIVING LEAD TO FINANCIAL BREAKTHROUGH

It is a good thing to be a giver. it is also wonderful to be a good person. As much as giving is good, as excellent as it sounds, I will like to let you know anyway that giving alone does not make anyone rich. As a matter of fact if you do not have a laid down principle when it comes to giving, senseless giving leads to poverty.

The rich and successful that is those with the abundance mindset make budgets and plans when it comes to giving. They do not just go ahead and distribute their income to whoever asks them for help or to whoever is in need like those with poverty mindset do, giving emotionally, forgetting that money is not emotional. They make a plan and set aside a percentage for giving. Your capital or the money you pay yourself is not meant for giving. If you do not make these plans properly, sooner or later you will join the multitude begging in the street.

Really you cannot help everyone. That is the reality of life. The more you build yourself and develop your financial capacity the more people you will be able to help. It is therefore advisable that you should pay more attention to developing your financial capacity to a point you will be able to help more people. If you do not do that and you allow your emotions to rule you, soon or later you will be out in the street among the group of those who are begging.

119

No matter what the need might be, the moment your budget for giving is emptied, do not touch your savings or the money you are paying yourself to supplement it. Let the need wait till the next month, and you can now make that need the first on your giving budget. Don't allow your emotions into it. Irrespective of who is involved, tell them to wait that you do not have the money now. The truth is you do not have the money. Know that any money you have kept for investment is no longer yours for spending. By so doing you will not feel guilty or think you lied by saying you don't have money. Because even God expects you to be a good steward of your money and the resources he has given to you. The number one way you become a good steward is not by giving but multiplying, you might want to read the parable of the talent in Matthew 25:14-30

> *"For the kingdom of heaven is like a man travelling to a far country, who called his own servants and delivered his goods to them. And to one he gave five talents, to another two, and to another one, to each according to his own ability; and immediately he went on a journey. Then he who had received the five talents went and traded with them, and made another five talents. And likewise he who had received two gained two more also. But he who had received one went and dug in the ground, and hid his lord's money. After a long time the lord of those servants came and settled accounts with them. "So he who had received five talents came and brought five other talents, saying, 'Lord, you delivered to me five talents; look, I have gained five more talents besides them.' His lord said to him, 'Well done, good and faithful servant; you were faith-*

ful over a few things, I will make you ruler over many things. Enter into the joy of your lord.' He also who had received two talents came and said, 'Lord, you delivered to me two talents; look, I have gained two more talents besides them.' His lord said to him, 'Well done, good and faithful servant; you have been faithful over a few things, I will make you ruler over many things. Enter into the joy of your lord. "Then he who had received the one talent came and said, 'Lord, I knew you to be a hard man, reaping where you have not sown, and gathering where you have not scattered seed. And I was afraid, and went and hid your talent in the ground. Look, there you have what is yours.' "But his lord answered and said to him, 'You wicked and lazy servant, you knew that I reap where I have not sown, and gather where I have not scattered seed. So you ought to have deposited my money with the bankers, and at my coming I would have received back my own with interest. Therefore take the talent from him, and give it to him who has ten talents. 'For to everyone who has, more will be given, and he will have abundance; but from him who does not have, even what he has will be taken away. And cast the unprofitable servant into the outer darkness. There will be weeping and gnashing of teeth."

I intentionally added this whole scripture to this chapter of the book, so you can read and have a better understanding of the explanation I am trying to give because most of us are worse than the servant with the one talent. At least he kept his one talent in a hole, but some of us would have spent it or given it out. The ones that will really want to be very religious and pleasing to God would have May be taken their own to church to give as offering and seed to prove to God how faithful they are. Imagine how God rebuked and punished the servant who returned the talent he gave him without multiplying it. So now I will like you to ask yourself, how about us who do not even have the original talent to return, neither did we multiply it because we gave it in church. How much do you think our punishment will be? This explains why a lot of people are poor in the body of Christ today.

Am I in any way against giving? Not at all, I am rather a giver to the core. But the truth of the matter remains that giving alone cannot make anyone rich. Without proper planning on how to give, manage and invest your resources, sooner or later, those resources will run out and you will not be in the position to give any more but will be with the masses who need help because you do not even have enough to satisfy your needs and wants. So it is prudent to be wise in your giving. You are to multiply your resources first before giving. The larger the multiplication of your resources, the more the capacity you will have to give. Let's take a look at some of the lessons we can learn from the parable of the talents.

FIVE LESSONS FROM THE PARABLE OF THE TALENTS

1. First, this parable teaches us that success is a product of our work.

In the book of Genesis we see that God placed Adam in the garden to work it and take care of it. We were made to work. As Christians we have a mission that our Lord expects us to accomplish in the here and now. Far too many evangelical Christians today see their salvation as simply a "bus ticket to heaven." They believe it doesn't matter what they do while they "wait for the bus." The Parable of the Talents teaches us what we are supposed to do while we await the return of our King. We are to work, using our talents to glorify God, serve the common good, and further God's kingdom. Biblical success is working diligently in the here and now using all the talents God has given us to produce the returns expected by the Master.

2. The Parable of the Talents teaches that God always gives us everything we need to do what he has called us to do.

Have you ever wondered what a talent is worth in today's dollars? It is hard to know for sure, yet whatever its exact value, in the New Testament a talent indicates a large sum of money, maybe even as much as a million dollars in today's currency. We are tempted to feel sorry for the servant who received only one talent, but in reality he received as much as a million dollars from the master and buried it in his back yard. He was given more than enough to meet the master's expectations.

Just as the master expected his servants to do more than passively preserve what has been entrusted to them, so God expects us to generate returns by using our talents towards productive ends. The servants were given enough to produce more – it is the same with the gifts God has given us. The Apostle Paul writes in Ephesians 2:10:

For we are God's handiwork, created in Christ Jesus to do good works, which God prepared in advance for us to do.

123

We seldom associate this verse with our work, but we should.

3. **The Parable of the Talents teaches that we are not all created equal.**

The most overlooked part of this parable is the second half of verse fifteen: the master gives to each servant talents, "…each according to his ability." The master understood that the one-talent servant was not capable of producing as much as the five-talent servant. We want to protest this as unfair. Yet we know this is true from our own experience. Diversity is woven into the fabric of creation. But even though we're not created equal in regard to the talents we're given, there is equality found in the Parable of the Talents. It comes from the fact that it takes just as much work for the five-talent servant to produce five more talents as it does the two-talent servant to produce two more talents. This is why the reward given by the master is the same. The master measures success by degrees of effort, as should we.

4. **The Parable of the Talents teaches that we work for the Master, not our own selfish purposes.**

The money that is given to the servants is not their own. The money they earn with the capital is not theirs to keep. The servants are only stewards of the master's investment, and it is the quality of their stewardship that the master seeks to measure. We should maximize the use of our talents not for our own selfish purposes, but to honor God. We know that we work in a fallen world. Because of the curse of sin, our work will be difficult. But we should feel satisfaction and joy from doing our best with what God has given us in the place where his providence puts us, seeking to succeed in order to honor him.

5. **The Parable of the Talents shows that we will be held accountable.**

The Parable of the Talents is not about salvation or works of righteousness, but about how we use our work to fulfill our earthly callings. It is about whole-life stewardship, or "Stewardship with a capital 'S." The unfaithful steward in this parable didn't so much waste the master's money – he wasted an opportunity. As a result, he was judged wicked and lazy. We are responsible for what we do for God with what we have been given, and one day we will be held responsible.

I believe now you can understand with me that the number one key to good stewardship is multiplication. You have to multiply whatever resources God has given to you. Be it in monetary form or not. But in the case at hand, I want us to stick to the monetary form of the resources. I do not think that master would have appreciated the servant with the ten talent, if he has just told the mater, master I gave all the resources you gave me to the church, or I gave them as gifts to those in need. What am I saying in essence? As much as giving is good, giving alone will not make you wealthy, neither is it a sign of good stewardship.

Multiply your resources through investment and plan your giving. He that fails to plan is planning to fail. I believe we are all familiar with that popular saying. Let's learn to be prudent in managing our resources. Don't let anyone, any pastor or church manipulate you into giving out of your budget. You are the one God gave your resources and you are the one He will ask for accountability. So manage your money properly and be a good steward for God by ensuring multiplication of your resources before giving or spending.

GOLDEN NUGGETS

1. Giving alone will not make you rich
2. Being good is not the key to wealth
3. Those with abundance mindset have their budget for giving
4. Those with poverty mindset give emotionally
5. Money is not emotional
6. You cannot help everyone.
7. The more you build your financial capacity the more people you will be able to help
8. Pay yourself first. And keep the money aside for investment
9. Get your golden goose that lays the golden egg
10. Be a good steward of the resources God has given you
11. Learn from the parable of the talents.
12. Good stewardship is not in giving but multiplication.

CHAPTER 16
HARD WORK ALONE CANNOT MAKE ONE RICH

In life we often think or we have been taught or told that success in life is all about hard work. As true and sincere as that may sound, look and seem, that to me is not the whole truth. Half-truth they say is as bad as no truth. If hard work alone is what brings success, then the laborers and truck drivers should be the most successful people. Or African continent should be one of the richest and most developed continents in the world because of how hard they work. But nothing is farther from the truth than this. The opposite is actually the case in these scenarios.

Hard work is not what makes one rich. The question should be what kind of hard work are you engaging in? Working hard with just physical strength will end you in penury. Those who become successful are those who work hard with their mind. Your mind should be the center and place of your hard work and not your fist. In other words you must learn to work smart.

Those with poverty mindset think that hard work is the secret to success. But is it? What does it mean to work hard anyway? People really struggle with ways to define it. Plus there seem to be more compelling factors at play. And if you neglect those fundamental factors that contribute to your overall success, you'll end up sabotaging it. Sometimes we forget the things that shape our journey the most are largely overlooked. But the people with the abundance mindset know better.

Consider the following factors, which demonstrate why hard work alone is not enough to archive success:

1. **Working smarter is more useful than working harder**

Working hard may be a waste of time, especially if you're not getting results. In fact, real estate mogul, Chris Leavitt, says that working smarter is a proactive strategy that sets pros apart. Very early in his career, he realized that time is a non-negotiable, non-renewable resource and people waste a lot of it. By working smarter, he discovered creative ways to achieve greater results without wasting time, compromising his integrity, or sacrificing the bottom-line.

2. **You need support**

Cultivating strong relationships is vital. No man is an island to himself, even when he wants to be. Serial entrepreneur, Richard Branson, says that success in business is all about making connections. And you would know, he's made a lot of great ones. Without the support of others who can help you to successfully pull projects forward, it can be very difficult to reach deadlines, relieve stress and expand your reach.

To be successful in business, you need to connect and collaborate and delegate. (Richard Branson)

3. **You need a compelling vision**

American life coach and self-help author, Tony Robbins, famously teaches that creating and executing the ultimate vision for your life matters: These concepts are critical to how you navigate the path to success. Despite humble beginnings and from a young age, Tony was very clear on how he wanted to live his life and created a compelling vision for how he could achieve it. It got him up early and kept him up late. His vision has translated into enormous career and financial success, as Tony has helped individuals all around the world to achieve peak performance and realize their wildest dreams. He was also named in Forbes magazine's 2007 "Celebrity 100" list, among other enviable accolades.

To create an extraordinary quality of life, you must create a vision that's not only obtainable, but that is sustainable. (Anthony Robbins)

4. You need to be consistent

Doing something once or twice — even when putting forth enormous effort — is usually not enough to yield results. But when you're consistent, more often than not, you'll see the fruits of your labor come to fruition. The Rock has mastered this principle. He knows that eating one healthy meal or doing one killer workout won't lead to the physique of your dreams. No matter what your goals may be, being consistent is the key to achieving them. There's simply no way around it. "Success isn't always about greatness. It's about consistency. Consistent hard work leads to success. Greatness will come."

5. Success requires sacrifice

Everyone wants to achieve success, but few are willing to sacrifice what it takes to get it. American Olympian, Gabrielle Douglas, knows a lot about sacrifice. After all, she's spent most of her life preparing for competitive gymnastics, a feat difficult for even the best of athletes. To be at her best, she needed to follow rigorous training regimens and an equally strict diet. She also spent a significant amount of time away from her family to train before participating in the 2012 Summer Olympics. Of course she's had plenty of good days, but she's also sacrificed a lot. Are you willing to sacrifice to get to the top?

I had to face a lot coming through this journey, a lot of sacrifices, difficulties, challenges, and injuries. (Gabrielle Douglas)

While hard work may be the default measurement for achieving success, there are clearly more compelling factors at play. And they shouldn't be overlooked. What other factors have you found relevant along the path to your success?

Am I in anyway against hard work? Not at all, I am a hard worker myself. I could pass for a workaholic. But what I am trying to let you know is that when it comes to financial success, hard work alone is not enough. Hard work alone will not make you rich. In addition to hard work, you must get the necessary knowledge needed to be able to make wealth and retain it. So if you are a hard worker, working in ignorance, you will live in penury like the lazy. Those who have the relevant knowledge and wisdom do not necessarily struggle with hard work without result. For you to have a result to show for your hard work, you must be knowledgeable in the area of financial freedom, in order to be able to work smartly and not just hard.

*People who work hard and peo-
ple who work smart have different measures of success.
(Jacob Morgan)*

Dear friends, I hope you now understand why hard
work alone is not enough. This is what those with abundance mindset know that those with poverty mindset do
not know. You will need to work smart by seeking for financial knowledge and applying it in your everyday life.
For me to drive this point home for us, I will like to end
this chapter with the life story of Davis.

Davis was a very hard worker who lived in the western part of African. He worked so hard but had very little
knowledge about financial laws or how they work. He
believed in saving and keeping his money in the bank,
but had very little knowledge that saving alone does not
make anyone rich. As inflation will take its toll on your
saved money and you become the looser at the end of
the day. He is not even aware of any such thing as inflation. But to cut the story short after 20 years of hard
work and savings, Davis was rest assured that he will not
lack anything in his retirement. But the greatest shock in
life hit Davis in a way he never expected when his bank
went bankrupt and closed down. I cannot begin to tell
you how devastating this happening was to Davis or how
he has to begin to live in penury because all his live savings are gone.

But this is just one segment of the story, even though
Davis's bank did not fold up; He would have still been a
looser at the end of the day, though not at this level. Savers are losers if they do not invest their saved money into
worthy businesses. The loss rate of leaving it dormant in

the bank is high because of inflation. You will agree with me that the worth of a 100 dollar bill 10 years ago is not same today anymore. It is therefore very vital to put your money to work and let your money work for you instead of working hard for money. That is what I call working smart financially, an act those with abundance mindset practice diligently. Their money is always at work for them, hence they are rich.

Seek for opportunities to invest. Your number one goal should be to seek knowledge on how you can put your money to work for you. What investment is safe for you to invest in and to stay aware of the vast opportunity that surrounds you daily. So you see, just hard work will not do that for you. You need to build relationship, seek financial experts to help you with direction in areas of investment. Seek advice from those who are already financially free. With all these in place, when you now add hard work to it, your door of riches and financial freedom will burst open to you. So if you must be rich and live in financial freedom, add to your hard work, knowledge and wisdom. Work smart not just hard. Join the club of those with abundance mindset and say goodbye to poverty mindset and poverty.

The benefits of working smart are just as profound: better health, often more money, a great work/life balance, more energy, a better self-esteem, exceptional productivity, and satisfaction with work. (Ron Alvesteffer)

GOLDEN NUGGETS

1. Hard work alone will not make you rich

2. Working smarter is more useful than working harder

3. You need to build relationships

4. You have to be consistent in what you do

5. You have to sacrifice today to reap the harvest you desire tomorrow.

6. Seek for opportunities to invest.

7. You loss when you leave your money dormant in the bank in the name of saving.

8. Stay aware of the vast opportunities that surround you on a daily bases by seeking knowledge.

9. You need to have a compelling vision.

10. Working hard with just physical strength will land you in penury

11. Your hard work should be done with your mind. That is working smart.

12. If physical hard work was the key to riches, then laborers should be the richest people on the earth.

CHAPTER 17
RICHES IS NOT DEPENDENT ON A TYPE OF CAREER

Those from the African decent will understand this phenomenon perfectly well, especially Nigerians my countrymen. Parents always choose specific careers for their children in order to secure their future. So it is never about what you love or what you are interested in, it is rather about what pays most. What career has the most job opportunities? There is nothing farther from the truth than this assertion. There is no specific career studied in school that provides a guarantee for riches. As a matter of fact, there are several millionaires and billionaires who do not even have a college degree. Some did not even make it from high school. Yet they are richer than most of the people in the society today with double and triple degrees in different professions.

Am I in anyway against schooling? Not at all, I am rather stating the fact and clearing the long lasting deception of associating riches with a type of career. Riches only come to those who know the laws of money. Everything in life is ruled and governed by different natural laws. Those who become rich or successful in life are those who have discovered these laws and are living by them.

As a matter of fact, those who choose a career in the hope that that career will give them the opportunity or privilege to a wide range of job opportunities have already lost their way to financial freedom. Having the

137

mentality of seeking for job, or looking for job safety can never make anyone truly rich. You only end up as a slave working all your life for money, always running the rat race.

Those with the abundance mindset are truly rich and they do not work for money. They have learnt to make their money work for them. The reason why anyone should go to school is to gain knowledge, develop and add value and worth to yourself not for the purpose of seeking for jobs. While you are busy thinking of what you can study to get a job, others are busy creating the jobs. It is these two different mentalities that make one person the employer and the other the employee. So you will spend all the years of your life in school, just to finish and start looking for a high paying job? From my point of view, that is the lowest level in the pyramid of securing riches and financial freedom. This is an awareness the people with abundance mindset have that those with poverty mindset lack.

Please know this, no one can ever be truly rich and enjoy financial freedom from a pay check. When you are living on a pay check you do not own your life, someone else is controlling your life for you. You cannot do what you want to do, when you want to do it and how you want to do it except you are ready to lose your job. Since you are so tied to your paycheck or salary, that you cannot afford to do without it, then you have to live by the rules of your employer and do his bidding for the rest of your working life until you are laid off. Is that really the kind of life you want to live? Is that the reason why you spent all your time and life in college? Is that really what you want for yourself? I don't think so, I think everyone will like to be in charge of their life and a master of their time while still making money.

If the latter is what you want, then continue reading this book and I will show you how you can do that in a short period of time. And live a healthy and fulfilled life in plenty and satisfaction while still in charge of your time and life.

Our school systems have really done a lot of injustice to us. The system of our education is wired in such a way that, students are taught to be job and salary conscious. Majority of the people that go to study in colleges are not studying because they want to develop themselves but because they want to be able to get a good job and have some salary security. This is the major reason 98 percent of the masses are in financial bondage while only 2 percent have financial freedom. For you to be free, you have to break from the shackles that have kept this 98 percent of the world population in bondage. And that bondage is ignorance to the laws of money.

It is time you began to seek to know what the rich know that has made them rich. You need to know what the people with the abundance mindset know that sets them ahead of those with the poverty mindset. It is time you began to acquire knowledge as regards to the principles behind financial freedom. Break free from the standard status-quo that our school system has deceived the masses to believe is the way to financial freedom and safety key. You are where you are today because of what you know and what you don't know.

Never buy into the white sold lies that your choice of career will guarantee you financial freedom. No! No!! No!!! It might guarantee you a job but definitely not financial freedom. The only thing that guarantees financial freedom is the laws of money you know and you have put into practice in your life. That is the only key to riches and financial freedom. This is exactly what the rich know that the poor don't know. The very edge the people with abundant mindset have over the people with poverty mindset.

How well do you know how to manage your money? Do you know how to put your money to work? Is money serving you or are you serving money. In order words, is money your servant or master? Before I go any further, let me let you know that money is a good servant but a bad master. So if money is your master, then know that you are heading for a life of poverty, lack and want. Always working and struggling to make ends meet. This is exactly what our schools train us for unfortunately, to work for money, to work to make a living, to live and be dependent on a pay check. So before you leave school, your mind is already programmed and trained not to think out of the box, but rather seek for financial freedom in getting a job. This is the greatest myth in our society today.

Know this: A college diploma is not a prerequisite for obtaining an absurd amount of wealth. Out of the 400 richest people in the U.S., 63 entrepreneurs don't have one–more than 15% of the list. With total U.S. student debt surpassing $1 trillion and unemployment pushing above 10% a budding entrepreneur might be tempted to skip university and instead enrol in the school of hard knocks.

Author Michael Ellsberg spent two years interviewing business titans who did just that for his book The Education of Millionaires (Penguin Group, 2011). Here are a few lessons gleaned from few billionaires who learned from life experience, not lecture halls. Inspired? Great! If not, you can always plop down six figures and head to campus.

1. Ruffin's last duty as someone else's employee was to repossess a monkey. He quit and founded a chain of stores, and later, hotels and casinos. "The advice I would give to young people? Quit your job. Don't work for anybody. You really can't make any money working for someone else." Phil Ruffin, Net worth: $2.4 billion.

2. "When these incredible tools of knowledge and learning are available to the whole world, formal education becomes less and less important. We should expect to see the emergence of a new kind of entrepreneurs who have acquired most of their knowledge through self- exploration." Sean Parker, Net worth: $2.1 billion.

My friends do not be deceived. The type of career you study is never a determinant factor to riches. If you doubt me, then I will like you to answer this question. The billionaires we have in our societies today that do not have a college degree or a high school certificate, what career determined their riches? I guess you already know the answer to that question. Now that we have been able to destroy this myth, let's now move together to the next chapter, where I will be treating the knowledge and the application of the laws of money. Please continue reading and you will get the long lasting answer you have been looking for.

GOLDEN NUGGETS

1. There is no specific career studied in school that provides a guarantee for riches
2. Our school systems have done us a lot of disservice
3. We are trained in our colleges to be job conscious
4. We are trained to be dependent on paychecks
5. You can never be financially free working for someone
6. The laws of money you know and are in operation in your life are the only guarantee to financial freedom
7. Are you serving money or money is serving you?
8. If money is your master, then you are heading for a life of poverty.
9. How well do you know how to manage your money?
10. As long as you work for paycheck you can never be in charge of your life and time
11. Those with abundance mindset do not go to school in other to get a job, but rather to create a job.
12. The people with poverty mindset go to school to get jobs and have salary security.

CHAPTER 18
THE KNOWLEDGE AND APPLICATION OF THE LAWS OF MONEY

I once had a very interesting conversation with a young man, who was complaining to me of how stingy his uncle was. He told me his uncle's lifestyle disgusted him so I was really interested in knowing why that was so. To my amazement I could not believe my ears when this young man started pouring out his grievances about his uncle's attitude. According to him, his uncle takes account of every penny he gives out, if he sends you on an errand he expects you to return the left over money no matter how small it is. He will bring you to account for it. He lives below his means and will hardly enjoy himself.

After his long tail of disappointment, he now paused and said, what is the essence of making money if not to spend it? There is no meaning to working hard for money and you cannot spend the money to enjoy yourself when you finally have it. To him his uncle was a very wicked man. I could not help but laugh at the ignorance of this young man, I finally told him that with this mindset you have, you can never be rich. That is the exact reason why you are struggling financially. Instead of critiquing your uncle, I would rather you go to him and ask him to teach you what he knows. It is what he knows that you don't know that is making you to beg him for money and not him begging.

How many people do you hear this kind of sorry tail from daily? This will make you understand why the masses live in poverty. The average person believes that money is meant to be spent. That ideology is a strong deviation from the law of money. Money is not meant to be spent. You might want to ask, if money is not meant to be spent, what then is money meant for? Good question, I will answer you. To answer this question I would like us to take a look and an inventory at the laws of money.

THE BASIC LAWS OF MONEY

The first law of money is MULTIPLICATION. The law of multiplication states that, before you can spend money, you must have multiplied that money at least three times. Money therefore is not meant for spending but for multiplication. The first thing that comes to your mind when money gets into your hands should not be what you want to buy or need to have. Your first line of thought should be how I can multiply this money to have tangible returns. How do I multiply what I have now? How do I increase this money to double and triple it?

Those who live by this law are the people who make it big time in life. They are the ones who put their money to work for them instead of working for money. They have learnt how to make money their servant. They are the master of money and as such are able to put their money into rightful use. They are not controlled by money, they control money. That is why the first thing they do is to multiply money not spend it. Those who are controlled by money go on shopping sprees or spending money the moment money gets into their hands. They cannot control their desires, their money controls that.

They continue to buy and spend money as long as the money is there and only get a break and rest when the money is finished. Just to resume from where they stopped when the next money comes in or they receive another pay check. Some people's case is even worse, they even go ahead to spend and buy on credit, even before the money arrives their hand it's already gone.

When you are living this kind of life, you are violating the first law of money and you can never be rich that way. You will continue to live from hand to mouth, from paycheck to paycheck which is actually the lifestyle majority of the masses live. Then you wonder why poverty is on the increase? The answer is not far-fetched. The people are ignorant of the laws of money. The quality of your life is directly proportional to the knowledge you have. You can never live better than what you know. Those with the abundance mindset know and practice the laws of money while those with poverty mindset are ignorant of it.

The second law of money is RETENTION. So many people do not know what it means to retain money. When it comes to money retention, savings alone is not enough. A lot of people say to themselves if I could just save huge amount of money in my bank account, then I can retire and live happily ever after. That is the greatest form of illusion in the 21st century. Have you ever heard that saying, "savers are losers"? Oh yes, you may have heard it or not, but that does not change the fact that this is true. Money that is just saved in the bank without being invested cannot be retained. Why, you might want to ask me? The answer is simple, INFLATION. Have you heard that word? Do you know what it means? For clarity sake, let's take a look at the meaning of the word inflation and how it negatively affects the retention of money through savings.

What is inflation?

To put it simply, inflation is the long term rise in the prices of goods and services caused by the devaluation of currency.

Inflationary problems arise when we experience unexpected inflation which is not adequately matched by a rise in people's incomes. If incomes do not increase along with the prices of goods, everyone's purchasing power has been effectively reduced, which can in turn lead to a slowing or stagnant economy. Moreover, excessive inflation can also wreak havoc on retirement savings as it reduces the purchasing power of the money that savers and investors have squirreled away.

For example, 1980 in the United States – just over 30 years ago – a new home in this country cost an average of $76,000, and the median income was $17,710 per year. Compare that to 2011, when even after the recent recession, the median home price stood at $139,000, and median household income was $50,233 per year according to the US Census Bureau.

Why the vast difference in prices? One word: Inflation. Like aging or weight gain, the effects of inflation are both gradual and profound. Inflation creeps up on us over time, and as we continue our normal spending and consumption habits, the almost imperceptible increase of consumer prices doesn't seem to make a huge difference in our day to day finances – which means it is all too often vastly underestimated.

But the effects of inflation are huge. And it doesn't just affect areas like our salaries and the cost of purchasing a new home. Inflation hits us from every angle. Food prices go up, transportation prices increase, gas prices rise, and the cost of various other goods and services skyrocket over time. All of these factors make it absolutely essential that you account for the huge impacts that inflation can have on your long-term savings and ability to fund your golden years of retirement.

The third law of money is INVESTMENT. Money is meant to be invested. For you to be able to retain the value of money, you have to be knowledgeable about investment. You have to learn to invest rightly in order for retention and multiplication to be actualized.

These three laws were the laws in operation in the parable of the talent. The one with the five talents was able to retain his money and multiplied it. The same thing happened in the case of the one with the two talents. But the one with the one talent was not able to retain his money talk more of multiplying it. Take note of the fact that even though he went to hide the money and did not spend it, he was not able to retain the money. The principle of inflation affected it and God rebuked him, He called him a wicked and lazy servant.

This is exactly the same thing that happens when we keep on saving money and leaving it in the bank without investing it. Such money can never retain its value.

BASIC PRINCIPLES OF MONEY

1. Money comes to those who know and abide by its principles. God made us to live by laws, not by miracles or mysteries.

2. The knowledge of the law of money is the key demand for wealth. To obtain this knowledge, find mentors, coaches, teachers, and partners for wealth.

3. The first thing to do with money is save.

4. Income does not determine wealth, knowledge does.

5. Minimize expenses.

6. Don't steal. Pay your tithes and taxes. For a secure future, pay all your debts.

7. Wealth comes by investment. Save in order to multiply the savings, retain by minimizing cost, and multiply by investment and production.

8. Don't listen to the dictates of money. It is a tool, a good servant but a bad master.

9. Wealth comes by working harder, longer or even wiser. It comes by applying principles, time, energy, your mind, and your money.

10. It is easier to obtain wealth in poor surroundings than in rich or developed surroundings with already-maximized potential, so never complain about your circumstances.

11. Ignore social expectations demanding a certain standard of social behaviours.

12. Money does not come because someone is good, spiritual or lucky. It comes to those who know and apply the principles of money. Proverb 6:6-11

13. There are no limits in life except those on the mind.

14. Don't keep liabilities. Keep only assets.

15. The reasons for failure in life are ignorance and laziness.

16. Do not despise the day of small beginnings.

Start with small savings.

17. The windows of heaven are open to send blessings, not money. God sends ideas and designs but he does not send money. Deuteronomy 8:18

18. Let God become your partner

19. Money comes by cultivating your land and producing goods and services. Genesis 2:15 says: *"The Lord God took the man and put him in the Garden of Eden to work it and take care of it"* (NIV).

20. God's blessing is important for enduring wealth without sorrow. God's blessing is the guard against evil. In proverbs 10:22, we are told, *"The blessing of the Lord makes one rich and he adds no sorry to it."* Never love money. Instead, love God, and you will be able to subdue money.

When you know these laws and principles of money, and you begin to put it into practice, applying these laws and principles in your everyday life, then riches will come your way. You will not need to be dependent on paycheck or salary anymore when you put this knowledge to work. This is exactly what the rich; those with the abundance mindset know that the poor or those with poverty mindset don't know. I will like us to end the chapter on this note:

> *If money is your hope for independence you will never have it. The only real security that a man will have in this world is a reserve of knowledge, experience, and ability (Henry Ford)*

GOLD NUGGETS

1. Money is not meant to be spent
2. First thing you do with money is save and then invest.
3. The knowledge of the law of money is the key demand for wealth.
4. Money is meant for multiplication (1st law of money)
5. Money is meant to be retained (2nd law of money)
6. Money is meant to be invested (3rd law of money)
7. Money is not meant for spending
8. Saving alone will not retain your money
9. Invest in other to beat inflation
10. Inflation affects money that is saved without investment
11. Money comes to those who know the laws of money
12. Money comes to those who practice the principles of money.

CHAPTER 19
SELF-FINANCIAL EDUCATION IS CONTINUOUS

Formal education will make you a living; self-education will make you a fortune (Jim Rohn)

The rich, those with the abundance mindset know that educating yourself financially should be a continuous process in your daily life and activities in order to stay up to date with the happenings around them and in the world, so as to be able to take advantage of every opportunity that comes their way, while the poor, people with poverty mindset seldom think of financial education, talk more of making it a daily routine. They are rather more concerned about seeking for jobs and looking for the jobs that pay more. This is one of the major disparities between the rich and the poor, the people with abundance mindset and the people with poverty mindset

Education should be a continuous process and our everyday lifestyle, so should financial education be. Buy books on finance and investments, do research, and attend financial seminars. Learn about the happenings in your economy; get knowledge on taxes, loans, credit cards etc. in order not to misuse the "vast opportunity" that is presented to the masses in the form of loans and credit cards and amass greater debt for yourself. Very few people in our present day society really have a full understanding of how their credit cards work.

151

Most people are just fascinated by the fact that they have credit cards and can afford to buy what they want without fully knowing the effect this is having on their income on the long run. Some people have ventured into taking loans that they did not have a full understanding of the interest rate and how it works for them or against them and this has led so many people to bankruptcy. So many people have become homeless and bankrupt because of lack of knowledge in financial management.

Financial illiteracy is like being in a rain storm and trying to jump in between the raindrops... eventually it all catches you at the same time. (Johnnie Dent Jr.)

So the value of financial education in our present time cannot be over emphasized. This is what those with the abundance mindset know that those with the poverty mindset don't know. Ignorance of financial management has made more people poor than bad economy has. Always remember this; you can never live better than you know. The quality of your life is directly proportional to the quality of your knowledge.

IMPORTANCE OF FINANCIAL EDUCATION

Finance touches us all, no matter what your occupation might be ,whether you are an expert in oil and gas, a programmer, a designer, a teacher, or a sales person, everyone is exposed to finance. The moment someone pays you for a service that you are providing or a product that you are selling, you enter the world of finance.

The question of what should be done with the money you earn is a fundamental one. How much should you spend on what, what portions should be saved, and where should you invest your savings?

The reputation of the finance industry in recent years has left much to be desired and in the aftermath of the great recession, there is a sense of mistrust among the general public. This is a psychological barrier for those who are seeking financial education or those who are interested in approaching financial planners. Nevertheless, as long as citizens are able to obtain two years' worth of income in an instant in the form of personal loans, and as long as credit cards are distributed like promotional brochures, it is important to break the psychological barrier and educate the public on how to be financially healthy and exercise prudence in the use of products that the financial industry offers.

Whenever financial education is mentioned, most people think of stocks, bonds, currencies, loans and credit cards. In reality, financial education, in its most basic form, is about managing and planning your expenses, your income and your future.

I would advocate for financial education to be given the same emphasis as the other core subjects, such as Biology or Physics, which are taught at school. Surely, knowing how to manage your money is as beneficial, later on in life, as lessons about photosynthesis and the mechanics of light reflections on concave mirrors.

If from a young age, our children are exposed to managing their allowances, perhaps on a spreadsheet or a piece of paper, recording their expenses and their income, or even encouraged to save for something they would like to buy, I believe it would produce a generation of financially healthy adults.

I was pleased to read that the Emirates Foundation and the Ministry of Education in the UAE have initiated plans to include a focus on budgeting and personal finance in the government school curriculum. This is, indeed, an excellent step in the right direction to develop the foundations of a financially literate country.

The next step is to build on these platforms and introduce the second phase of financial education, which I believe should be focused on developing awareness of behavioral biases towards financial decisions.

In conversations with investors in the region, I have noted several behavioral biases. One of the most common behavioral biases is herding, where individuals mimic the actions, whether rational or irrational, of a larger group. For example, some investors make their investment decisions on stocks of companies without studying their financial statements properly, but simply because the market is "rallying."

Another prevalent behavioral bias in our society is confirmation bias, in which investors seek out information that supports their original idea about an investment and ignore information that contradicts it. Other common behavioral biases I have encountered include Mental Accounting bias, in which individuals separate their money based on subjective criteria. For example, some will have a special savings account set aside for a particular purpose earning 3 per cent a year, while still carrying substantial credit card debt accruing interest at 36 per cent annually.

In this case, the most logical action would be to use the savings to pay off the debt. This seems simple enough, but in reality, the majority of people do not behave in this way.

The third phase of a well-rounded financial education system should address the responsible use of debt, such as loans and credit cards, reading and understanding the basics of financial statements and investments, which would include the characteristics of various asset classes, their risk and reward relationship, and the importance of exercising due diligence before making investment decisions.

I believe this three-phased approach to financial education in schools and educational institutions, which covers theoretical and practical applications of budgeting and personal finance, behavioral biases, debt, financial statements, and investments, represents the cornerstones of a financially healthy society that will yield a future of greater prosperity.

Your economic security does not lie in your job; it lies in your own power to produce- to think, to learn, to create, to adapt. That's true financial independence. It's not having wealth; it's having the power to produce wealth. It's intrinsic. (Stephen R. Covey)

In order to be rich and live in financial freedom, you must therefore seek to know what the rich knows. You must get financial knowledge, pursue self-education and stay up to date with the economical happenings in your environment. Live in the consciousness of the fact that education is meant to be a continuous process if you seek to have financial freedom. This is exactly what the people with the abundance mindset do that those with poverty mindset don't do.

GOLDEN NUGGETS

1. Financial self-education is continuous
2. Stay aware of the opportunities around you
3. Financial education is a necessity and optional irrespective of your profession.
4. Financial education should be taught in our institutions
5. Financial education should be a part of our school curriculum
6. Financial education, in its most basic form, is about managing and planning your expenses, your income and your future.
7. Financial education system should address the responsible use of debt.
8. Children should be taught financial education early in life
9. Everyone needs financial education
10. Don't be in a haste to take credit cards without proper education.
11. Get the full information you need before taking any loan.
12. Financial education prepares you for a life of financial freedom.

CHAPTER 20
THEY KNOW THAT COMFORT IS A REWARD OF PATIENCE IN DISCOMFORT

While the poor, those with poverty mindset run after comfort, the rich, those with abundance mindset know that comfort is a reward of patient in discomfort. Their number one pursuit is not comfort; they have learnt to delay gratification in order to pursue financial freedom. The reverse is the case for the poor. They pursue comfort and will rather borrow or buy on credit to get the desired comfort they need. You don't have to eat your future today just because you have appetite or you desire to live in comfort. Rather discipline yourself in discomfort today in order to have a larger scale of comfort in the future.

Over 80 percent of Americans live on credit. They buy a house on credit, car on credit, furniture on credit etc. it is a very wrong ideology to borrow or take credit for consummation. If you must take credit, or be in debt, it has to be for an investment that will give you returns to pay off your credit in due time while still having your profit. This is the kind of debt I call good debt. Anything other than investing and multiplication of money is not worth taking credit for. Stop buying liabilities with credit card. Living this kind of lifestyle is mortgaging your future before you even get into it. It is better to learn to live within your means.

But unfortunately, this is not always the case with the poor. They try to live at the same level with the rich without knowing how long the rich had to suffer in discomfort before having the comfort that they want to have immediately now without working hard for it. You have to pay the price for the luxury you wish to have. Learn not to buy what you cannot afford just because you have a credit card at your disposal. That is a big trap leading you headlong into financial bondage. Learn to curtail your spending, let delayed gratification be your key words.

We live in a culture that has taught us that instant gratification is okay. In fact, it's more than okay, it's how most people function. Need a snack? Go to a nearby vending machine or convenience store. Need a new car? Go down to the dealership and drive away in a newly leased vehicle the same day. Need money quickly? Get a payday loan. This can have a disastrous effect on our financial situation. If we're programmed to spend, spend, spend, how can we fight against this culture of instant gratification and move toward delayed gratification for the sake of our wallets?

If you're wondering why delayed gratification is a good idea, consider this: you'll be saving all the money you otherwise would have spent on trivial things. If you've been a victim of buyer's remorse lately, then delayed gratification could be your solution. Delayed gratification also leads to more mindful spending because it forces you to evaluate whether or not you really want (or need) something. Do you want to embrace delayed gratification? Then these 3 methods might be of help:

1. Set a Spending Limit

Before you can embrace delayed gratification, it's a good idea to set some boundaries regarding your spending. While your ultimate goal should be to avoid all impulse purchases, if you give in to instant gratification a lot, you can start with a spending limit and work your way down.

Everyone's number is going to look different, but figure out an amount you think is appropriate for you to second-guess the purchase you're contemplating. Maybe that's anything above £40 for you. That means if you're eyeing a new pair of shoes for £50, you should stop and use one of the strategies below to help you embrace delayed gratification.

2. Sleep on It

Sleeping on a decision is one of the easiest ways to delay your spending and help you "forget" about your wants. It also gives you a self-imposed time limit to figure out if the purchase is worth it. Going back to that shoe example, you might find that because you were out shopping, you were naturally in the mood to spend. After having removed yourself from that situation, and spending a day thinking about it, you might realize you don't actually want those shoes after all. Delayed gratification is all about taking a moment to step away from the temptation to buy and reflect in a rational way instead.

3. List out the Pros and Cons

Sometimes waiting it out isn't enough to deter you from a purchase, but you're still on the fence. Making a list of the pros and cons of a purchase can help you decide whether or not you should spend your money. Let's say you really want a new phone, but the one you currently have is still functioning just fine. Rationally, you know that you don't need a new phone, but all the hype surrounding its release is hard to ignore. Make a list. What are the pros to getting a new phone? Does it have better options available? Is it faster? Will you be more productive with it?

What are the cons? The cost? Possibly renewing your contract with your provider (thus making it harder to get out of down the road)? Having to get used to a new operating system? After jotting down the pros and cons, you should have a better idea of what to do with your money.

4. Keep Your Savings Goals In Mind

Another strategy for delayed gratification is keeping your savings goals in mind. This method works extremely well to combat smaller impulse purchases as well as lofty purchases that will make a bigger dent in your bank account. If you haven't already defined what your savings goals are, then do so now. What are you saving your money for, retirement, investments, a vacation, paying off debt etc.?

Now when you're faced with the temptation to spend, ask yourself: "Is it worth giving up X amount of money toward my goal of saving for _____?" "Which do I want more, a new pair of shoes, or an investment to yield greater returns or a vacation to Italy?" Hopefully this will help put your potential purchases in perspective.

What If You Really Do Want Something?

Maybe you've put all the above methods to use, but find that you still actually want to buy something. That's fine, but there's no reason to go out and buy it immediately if you can't afford it. Don't fall into the trap of paying for things with credit card if you don't have the funds available. You'll end up paying more because of interest. Instead, do the smart thing and save up for purchases. You should actually always be saving – this way, when you find something you want to buy, you can buy it right when you make the decision instead of having to wait.

I for one have been in positions when I spent so much to buy things I didn't necessarily need. For example, in my house after we built it, I spent thousands of dollars buying television sets for every room in the house. My house is a mansion, a 60 bed room house. So I bought television for each and every of those rooms. Only to discover that I did not need to buy all these televisions. In my house I cannot remember the last time we watched television, yet I spent so much on buying all of it. So it is with most of us, for most of the things we buy.

Because of the adverts, we are most times prone to buying things out of emotions, excitements and not necessarily out of needs. Most of these things we buy are liabilities that will only take more money from our pockets thereby leaving us with empty wallets at the end of the day. In order to be able to escape from buying when our emotions are rising, practicing delayed gratification is the only way out for us. The only power of deliverance that could save us or set us free from the manipulative adverts targeting to leave our pockets empty is delayed gratification.

Delayed gratification therefore is one of the major keys to financial freedom, because delayed gratification will definitely put your spending in check, thereby helping you to have more income to invest and more returns to your pocket. This is what those with abundance mindset practice that those with poverty mindset don't practice. Hence they are ahead of them financially and live in financial freedom, while they live in financial bondage. If only we would learn to put our spending in check, if only we would learn to delay gratification, we will be able to stay out of debt and say farewell to financial slavery.

Let your goal for financial freedom be your constant reminder of controlling your spending. Let it help you to live within your means, even though it means a temporal discomfort today in order to have a permanent comfort tomorrow. Delay your gratification. Take a lesson from the rich and pay the price for the luxury you want to have in the future today.

GOLDEN NUGGETS

1. To pursue financial freedom you must learn to delay gratification.
2. It is ok to live in temporal discomfort, while building a future of permanent comfort.
3. Never borrow for consummation
4. If you must borrow, let it be for investment.
5. Live within your means
6. Don't pursue comfort at the expense of financial capacity
7. Pursue financial freedom and comfort will follow
8. Don't buy things out of emotions
9. Always keep your saving goals in mind
10. Think more of the future comfort you will have if only you can control you desires for immediate gratification.
11. You do not need most of the things you want to buy.
12. Learn to sleep over a purchase you desire to make and you will discover if you really need it or not.

PART 5

THE DIFFERENT ATTITUDES TO MONEY BY THE POOR/RICH

CHAPTER 21
THE POOR WASTE MONEY (FOOLS)

*Poverty has many roots, but
the tap root is ignorance
(Lyndon B Johnson)*

What do you mean by the poor waste money? How can they possibly waste what they don't have? Are they not poor because they don't have money? This and many more questions might be what could be running through your mind right now as a result of this topic or the tittle of this chapter. But as inconsistent as you might think this statement is; sadly it is the truth. The poor waste money and I will tell you how.

I Spent 5 Years Studying Poor People and Here Are 4 Destructive Money Habits They Had said - Thomas C. Corley

Your money habits can make you rich or put you in the poor house. According to a recent study by Brown University, in which nearly 50,000 families were surveyed, most of the habits we pick up in life come from our parents (Brown Study). This includes money habits. If your parents had bad money habits it is likely those habits rubbed off on you. But in order to change bad money habits you need to first become aware of them. Below are some destructive money habits that I uncovered in my five year Rich Habits study that will put you in the poor house unless you eliminate them:

Gambling Habits – Gambling is not a sound plan to lift you out of poverty. Gambling relies on random luck.

The odds of winning Powerball are 1 in 175 million. That's basically zero. Seventy-seven percent of the poor admitted to playing the lottery regularly vs. 6% of the rich. But it's not just the lottery they gamble their money on….. 52% of the poor admit that they gamble on sports at least once a week vs. 16% of the wealthy.

Time Wasting Habits – Time is money. The rich, (people with abundance mindset) understand this. Sixty-five percent of the rich created at least three streams of income during their lives. Conversely, the poor, (people with poverty mindset) all relied on one stream of income. They didn't invest their time wisely in building their careers or building a side business. In my study, I uncovered many time wasters the poor engaged in that ultimately cost them money: Seventy-seven percent of the poor admitted to watching more than one hour of TV each day and their preference? Reality TV wins hands down. Seventy-eight percent of the poor watch reality TV shows. The rich, on the other hand, are not big on TV. Sixty-seven percent watch less than an hour each day and it's not reality TV that they tune in to. Only 6% watch reality TV. Another time waster is the Internet. Seventy-four percent of the poor in my study spent more than an hour each day on the Internet. These days that means Facebook, Twitter, Instagram, Snapchat or YouTube. Conversely, 63% of the rich spent less than an hour each day on the Internet. This freed up more time to read for self-education. While many of the poor in my study said they read regularly, 79% admitted that they read strictly for entertainment. Only 11% of the rich said they read for entertainment. Instead, they focused their reading on self-education: biographies of successful individuals, career-related reading, self-help, history and money matters. When you're wasting your time watching TV, on social media or reading for entertainment it leaves little time to do productive things like reading to learn, building relationships with other success-minded individuals via networking or volunteering or building a side business. Time does not discriminate. Everyone gets twenty four hours, rich or poor. The rich simply choose to spend their time differently, doing things that are productive. This is what differentiates those with poverty mindset from those with abundance mindset.

Bad Spending Habits – The rich in my study made a habit of tracking their spending in the early days of building their wealth. It's easy to lose sight of where your money is going. If you don't have a lot of money you need to get into the habit of tracking every penny. The poor in my study didn't. I uncovered certain poor spending habits that held the poor back in life: Ninety-three percent admitted that they did not budget their spending. Sixty-six percent admitted that they were not frugal with their money. They had a bad habit of making spontaneous purchases with their money. Oftentimes, this required them to use credit cards. Eighty-eight percent of the poor in my study had over $5,000 in revolving credit card debt. Sixty-nine percent used those credit cards to purchase big ticket items. And 77% had multiple credit cards. Conversely, 92% of the rich relied on one and only one credit card. Eighty-eight percent of the poor never shopped at a goodwill store in their lives. Many goodwill stores sell high quality clothing. The clothes may require some minor tailoring but, otherwise, you're getting real value at a steep discount. Sixty-eight percent of the poor said they don't use coupons. Why would you pay more for food than you have to? Every dollar you save is one less dollar you have to earn. Sixty-one percent of the poor did not own their homes but they rented them, while 100% of the rich owned their homes. When you don't own your home, you are unable to build home equity, which comes in handy when you retire or to help your kids with college costs.

Poor Savings Habits – Only 5% of the poor in my study saved 10% of their income. None saved 20% of their income. Conversely, 94% of the rich in my study saved 20% or more of their income. Many of the millionaires in my study started out poor and did not have large incomes during their lives, so this was a habit they adopted while they were still poor. Fifty-one percent were small business owners who watched what they spent in order to enable them to save money. They then invested their savings, as well as the investment income generated by their savings. After many years, their savings and investments compounded, eventually turning them into self-made millionaires. It wasn't easy but they did it. You can too! You just need a plan. You need to bite the bullet and save 10% or more of your income and then invest your savings wisely.

Building wealth takes time. It doesn't happen overnight. It took the average millionaire in my study thirty-two years to become rich. The younger you are the more time you have to build wealth. That's only possible if you eliminate destructive money habits and adopt sound money habits.

From the above research, you definitely have a clear understanding of how the poor waste their money. The poor are not necessarily poor because of the lack of money; they are poor because they lack initiatives. They are mostly ignorant of the laws and principles of money. Hence they live a life of constant waste. Waste of their money, waste of their time and a total waste of their creativity. The result is always a life of poverty and lack.

> *Empty pockets never held anyone back. Only empty heads and empty hearts can do that.*
> *(Norman Vincent Peale)*

You cannot choose to live on luxury when you cannot afford it and you are not ready to pay the price for it. Living a life of instant gratification, buying and spending on what you don't need is the root and express way to a life of lack. This is exactly what the poor do. The poor buy liabilities with their money. The rich spend their money on assets. The saving culture is far-fetched among the poor. As long as you continue to consume all that you earn, be rest assured that you cannot win your battle over poverty. Those with the abundance mindset have learnt the skills and acquired the knowledge of how to spend their money and time wisely, while those with the poverty mindset are ignorant in this area.

GOLDEN NUGGETS

1. The poor waste money
2. The poor have a lifestyle of gambling
3. The rich understand the value of time
4. The poor waste time
5. Building wealth takes time, it does not happen overnight
6. The rich have a good spending habit, they track their every penny.
7. The poor are careless with their spending. They do not have track record of their money.
8. Your money habit can either make you rich or poor
9. Poverty has many roots, but the tap root is ignorance
10. The rich are big on saving and investment.
11. The poor are small on saving and hardly invest
12. The rich spend their money on assets. The poor spend their money on liabilities.

CHAPTER 22
THE MIDDLE CLASS SPEND MONEY (MEDIOCRE)

The number one problem of the middle class is the love for comfort. They live for comfort and are not ready to accept discomfort as part of the price to pay in order to have financial freedom. The rich on the other hand, do the exact opposite.

Very few people in the middle class really understand the mindset of the richest people. After all, if they did, they would be among the top earners as well. We've all heard the remarks: Rich people are lucky, rich people had an unfair advantage, rich people are crooks, rich people are selfish, etc. These are mostly empty statements with little proof to back them up. Yes, the rich think and act differently from everyone else, and the differences are as extreme as they are numerous. See some areas in which the rich think totally different from the middle class.

1. **The rich are comfortable being uncomfortable.**

Most people just want to be comfortable. Physical, psychological, and emotional comfort is the primary goal of the middle-class mindset. The wealthy, on the other hand, learn early on that becoming a millionaire isn't easy, and the need for comfort can be devastating. They learn to be comfortable while operating in a state of ongoing uncertainty. The great ones know there's a price to pay for getting rich, but if they have the mental toughness to endure temporary pain, they can reap the harvest of abundant wealth.

It's not comfortable for a millionaire in the making to forge ahead when everyone around him/her is negative, cynical, and unsupportive, yet those who can push forward are rewarded with riches for the rest of their lives.

> *Be willing to be uncomfortable. Be comfortable being uncomfortable. It may get tough, but it's a small price to pay for living a dream. (Peter McWilliams)*

It's comfortable to work a "safe" job. It's comfortable to work for someone else. The middle class think being comfortable means being happy, but the rich realize that extraordinary things happen when we put ourselves in uncomfortable situations. Starting your own business is a risk and risks can be uncomfortable, but a little risk is what it takes to create wealth and achieve superior results.

Step out of your comfort zone. Look at all your options. You will have to be at least a little uncomfortable if you want to become rich. You might even have to fail and that's great, because if you're not failing, you're not doing much. Make a list of the five things you must do today that are uncomfortable but will help you build your financial fortune.

2. The rich dream about the future.

Most of us grew up listening to stories of the good old days, when the world was a kinder, gentler place. The music was better, athletes were tougher, and business people were honest. This tradition of the masses is handed down from generation to generation while its purveyors have no idea how insidious and destructive it is. People who believe their best days are behind them rarely get rich, and they often struggle with happiness and depression.

The rich are future-oriented and optimistic about what lies ahead. They appreciate and learn from the past while living in the present and dreaming of the future. Self-made millionaires get rich because they're willing to bet on themselves and project their dreams, goals, and ideas into an unknown future. Much of their planning time is spent clarifying goals that won't be realized for years, yet they patiently and painstakingly plan and dream of what their future will look and feel like.

3.   The middle class live above their means, the rich live below.

There is no dignity quite so impressive, and no one independence quite so important, as living within your means. (Calvin Coolidge)

You won't catch the average millionaire in a $100,000 car or a multi-million dollar home. The rich don't spend their money on depreciating liabilities, they spend their money on appreciating assets and they live below their means. On average, the rich drive cars that are a few years old and they don't buy them new, according to studies done in the book "The Millionaire Next Door." Even if they can "afford" that fancy new Escalade, they usually don't buy it. Remember, if you earn $1,000,000/year and you spend $1,000,000/year, you're still broke.

4. The rich are more confident.

The negative projections and derogatory labels placed on the rich are endless. One of the most common is that the rich are cocky, arrogant people who think they're better than everyone else. The truth is successful people are confident because they repeatedly bet on themselves and are rarely disappointed. Even when they fail, they're confident in their ability to learn from the loss and come back stronger and richer than ever. This is not arrogance, but self-assuredness in its finest form.

The wealthy have an elevated and fearless consciousness that keeps them moving towards what they want, as opposed to moving away from what they don't want. This often doubles or triples their net worth quickly because of the new efficiency in their thinking. Eventually they begin to believe they can accomplish anything, and this becomes a self-fulfilling prophecy. As they move from success to success, they create a psychological tidal wave of momentum that gets stronger every day, catapulting their confidence to a level so high it is often interpreted as arrogance.

5. The middle class climb the corporate ladder, the rich own the ladder.

The richest people in the world look for and build networks; everyone else looks for work. (Robert Kiyosaki)

The middle class tend to work for someone else. They have a job, a career. Upper middle class tend to be self-employed. They own a job. The rich tend to own the business. They own that corporate ladder that the middle class are busy working up. The rich understand that they need more people working for them to earn more money. The rich understand the power of passive income.

6. **The rich believe money is about freedom.**

Among the many money issues misperceived by the general public is the notion that acquiring great wealth is more about showing off than creating choices. While money certainly brings status, it's acquired mostly for the purpose of attaining personal liberty. It's impossible to be truly free without wealth. The middle class is controlled by employment, government, and other entities with superior resources that dictate what they can and can't do. It's tough to make a moral stand for freedom when you're worried about making your next mortgage payment.

Rich people can afford to stand up and fight oppression. They can afford to buy their way out of unhealthy work environments, bad bosses, and other unpleasant situations. They have the means to enlist the best doctors when they get sick, and they are able to make themselves as comfortable as possible when they can't get well. When they want to raise money for business, politics, or charity, a few phone calls to their rich friends is all it takes. If they need more money, they throw a party or host an auction and charge $1,000 a ticket. The examples of how much money buys freedom are endless. Start thinking about the freedoms you'll gain when you are wealthy!

7. **The middle class work to earn, the rich work to learn.**

When you are young, work to learn, not to earn. (Robert Kiyosaki)

The middle class are easily persuaded to change jobs when someone offers more money. The rich understand that working isn't about the money, especially in the early years. It's about developing the skills and traits you need to develop to become rich. That may mean working a sales job to better understand the world of selling. Or it could mean you work at a bank to better understand accounting. If you want to be rich, you should be working to learn the skills you need to become rich. Most rich people didn't get there by earning a high salary.

8. The rich carefully monitor their associations.

People with high-level formal education like to associate with the academic elite. Physically fit people enjoy spending time with others who are fit. Religious people like to have fellowship with people of faith. And rich people like to associate with others who are rich. Like attracts like, yet the wealthy are often criticized for having a closed inner circle that is almost impossible to break into unless you are rich. Successful people generally agree that consciousness is contagious, and that exposure to people who are more successful has the potential to expand your thinking and catapult your income. We become like the people we associate with, and that's why winners are attracted to winners.

In other segments of society this is accepted, but the rich have always been lambasted for their predisposition to engage the company of people with similar financial success. Millionaires think differently from the middle class about money, and there's much to be gained by being in their presence. Set a goal to double the amount of time you spend with people who are richer than you.

Who knows, it might just make you rich. The middle class are friends with everyone, the rich choose wisely

It's better to hang out with people better than you. Pick out associates whose behaviour is better than yours and you'll drift in that direction. (Warren Buffett)

The rich understand that when you surround yourself with successful people, your own success will follow. Likewise, surrounding yourself with unsuccessful people tends to have the anticipated effect. Your income is usually the average of the incomes of your three closest friends. If you want to earn more, hang around people who earn more. It's all about aligning your mindset with the mindset of successful people. If you want to be rich, you have to think rich.

9. The middle class have things, the rich have money.

Too many people spend money they haven't earned, to buy things they don't want, to impress people that they don't like. (Will Rogers)

Back to the fancy cars and big houses, that's where much of the middle class spend their money. Drive through a middle class neighbourhood and you will usually see brand new cars, expensive landscaping and high-dollar homes. The rich understand that to become wealthy, you have to want money more than you want things. If you keep buying things, your money will keep going with them. It's funny how that works. For example,

Warren Buffett still lives in the same home he bought in 1958. And he only paid $31,500 for it.

Stop buying things and start focusing on keeping, saving and investing the money you earn. If you are a shopaholic, start shopping for assets. Become interested in investing, then look for bargains on stocks and businesses instead of shoes and electronics. That being said, it's not all about saving your money.

10. The middle class focus on saving, the rich focus on earning

Your greatest asset is your earning ability. Your greatest resource is your time.
(Brian Tracy)

Saving is important. Investing may be more important, but earning is the foundation of both. You understand that you need to save and invest, but to really achieve extravagant goals with them, you need to earn more. The rich understand this and work on creating more avenues to earn and earning more with the avenues they have. If you really want to become rich, work on your earning ability, not your saving ability.

11. The middle class are emotional with money, the rich are logical

Only when you combine sound intellect with emotional discipline do you get rational behaviour.
(Warren Buffett)

Steve Siebold interviewed over 1,200 of the world's wealthiest people over the past 30 years for his book

"How Rich People Think", and according to him there are more than 100 differences in how rich people look at money compared to the middle class. One of the key differences he found was that the middle class see money through the eyes of emotion, but the rich see money through the eyes of logic. Making emotional financial decisions will ruin your finances. Warren Buffett explains that investing has much more to do with controlling your emotions, than it has to do with money. Emotions are what cause people to buy high and sell low. Emotions create dangerous business deals. Leave emotions out of this and turn to logic.

12. **The middle class underestimate their potential, the rich set huge goals.**

Set your goals high, and don't stop till you get there.
(Bo Jackson)

The middle class set goals some times. It's the capacity of the goals that differ from the middle class to the rich. The middle class set safe goals that are easily obtainable. The rich set goals that seem impossible, difficult or crazy. But they know they are achievable. It all comes back to having the proper mindset.

When you're setting your goals, ask yourself if they could be bigger. Ask yourself if that's really all you can do or if you can do more. I think you can do more.

13. **The middle class believe in hard work, the rich believe in leverage.**

It is much easier to put existing resources to better use than to develop resources where they do not exist.
(George Soros)

183

Hard work is a necessity for all of us. If you want to reach the top (whatever that may be for you), you've got to put in the work. The problem is that hard work alone will rarely make you rich. You can't become rich by doing it all yourself. You have to use leverage to truly become rich and stay that way. Leverage works in many ways, from outsourcing to investing. The more leverage you can incorporate, the more time you will free up to work on the things that really matter in your business and your life. Some differences between the middle class and the rich are vast, while others may seem simple and minor. The fact is that if you want to become rich, you have to think like the rich and do the things the rich do.

GOLDEN NUGGETS

1. The middle class spend money.
2. Money is not meant to be spent
3. The middle class have things, the rich have money
4. Money is not emotional, it is logical.
5. Don't spend the money you haven't earned
6. The rich understand that when you surround yourself with successful people, your own success will follow.
7. The rich understand that to become wealthy, you have to want money more than you want things
8. Emotions are what cause people to buy high and sell low.
9. Emotions create dangerous business deals.
10. Leave emotions out of business and money, rather turn to logic. That is the language of money
11. You can't become rich by doing it all yourself.
12. You have to use leverage to truly become rich and stay rich.

CHAPTER 23

THE RICH INVEST AND MULTIPLY MONEY (WISE)

There is definitely something the rich, people with abundance mindset know that the poor, people with poverty mindset don't know. That one thing is their understanding and response to money. The rich know and understand that money is not meant for spending. They know that it is one thing to make money; it is another thing to maintain money and a totally different ball game to grow money. It is this understanding that has kept them separate from the poor and middle class. This understanding is the basis of the differentiation between these classes of people.

I know most times we think that it is hard work, but I bet to disagree with you. Because in most cases those who work the hardest are the middle class, the rich do not necessarily work harder than the middle class. There is something they do better, they work smarter. They work hard with their mind not their fist or legs. They know and live by the principles and laws of money. They are the master of their money and know just how to put their money to work for them, in order for them not to work for money.

Let's take a look at some different ways the rich do things differently and how they handle their money differently. If you want to be rich, then you must know what the rich know.

LESSONS FROM THE RICH

The first thing the rich know about money is that having it is one thing, the challenge comes in maintaining it or better still growing it so as to have a constant supply of the same. Only the rich seem to have mastered the art of multiplying their money such that they keep having it. To grow your money, you need to know what the rich do and how they do it.

1. A Penny Saved Is A Penny Earned

When you resist the temptation to spend on something you would otherwise do without, definitely you have earned that money. Not spending is same as earning. The money saved can then be used to invest, ultimately creating an income stream. So make sacrifices in the manner you spend and you will increase your income.

2. Spread Your Risks.

The rich know only too well how risky it is to put all your eggs in one basket. According to "Investopedia", it is foolish to put all your money in one investment. Diversification is the song of the rich because this way, they are assured of returns should one investment go wrong. An example could be the stock market, treasury bonds, real estate or better still farming. It is also critical to know that while investing in the stock market; it's advisable not to concentrate in one industry.

3. Invest In Appreciating Assets

The rich know how unwise it is to put money in deprecating assets like vehicles and machinery. Wherever your money is invested, it should be able to give you more than what you put in. Land, property, bonds are some of the assets that more often than not guarantee you more than what was invested should you want to exit the investment.

4. Avoiding Complex Investments

If the investment is difficult to understand, stay away from it. The rich know it's wise to stay away from an investment in which they cannot control the risks involved. In most cases, complex investment are sold to the masses, most of whom don't understand them, the rich never put their money in an investment they do not understand. The simple logic here is, if it is complex to understand, it is probably complex to make money from it too.

5. Stay Awake To An Investment Opportunity

Opportunity, they say, favors a prepared mind. The rich are always on the lookout for investment opportunities. They understand only too well that money has to be multiplied and they don't settle for what they already have. They are always listening to new ideas on making money, even if they don't like the idea.

HOW THE RICH MANAGE THEIR MONEY DIFFERENTLY THAN EVERYBODY ELSE

The rich people manage their money differently than everyone else. They make different decisions and have an entirely different way of thinking about money. But even if you're not rich, you can still manage your money like the rich do. This is the first step towards becoming rich.

1. **The wealthy forget about instant gratification.**

Humans are wired for instant gratification. We love it. But evolution made us that way long before our modern monetary system came about. The desire for instant gratification doesn't help us when we're trying to become wealthy; it hurts us. Stop making decisions that will make you happy now, but mess up your future wealth.

2. **The wealthy understand the difference between wants and needs.**

"We need a bigger house," you may say. Don't confuse wants with needs. A common mistake poor people make is to disguise wants as needs as a way to justify them. Then you feel better about making a poor financial choice. Wealthy people understand the difference between what you need and what you want. Know the difference between a want and a need and don't lie to yourself about it.

3. **The wealthy invest automatically.**

There are ways to automate investment, such as payroll deduction to a retirement account, which is great, but the mentality of investing is more important. Automatic or not, wealthy people believe so strongly in investing that they do it as habitually as you brush your teeth in the morning. There's no question about how much they invest, they know how much they must invest because they set goals (we're going to get to that) and know how much money they need to reach those goals.

4. **The Rich understand the cost of debt.**

"What are the monthly payments?" is what poor people ask when considering a car purchase. That's the wrong question. A better question is "what is this car really going to cost me?" When you multiply the monthly payment by the number of months of the loan, you'll see a shocking number that's way more than the cost of the car and that's before depreciation, taxes and other expenses. This is the number you have to be comfortable with. Better yet, be uncomfortable with it and keep your old car.

5. **The Rich start with a goal and work backward.**

Know what you want and what it's going to take to get it. If you don't know what you want, you'll get something that's the result of a bunch of decisions made for instant gratification. Most likely that will be poverty. Decide what you want your life to be like, figure out how much that will cost and do exactly what you need to do to get there.

Josh Simon, 28-year-old real estate millionaire, says,

Figure out how you would like to live in retirement, come up with a number, then work on a strategy to realize that number.

6. **The Rich live within their means.**

The great thing about investing automatically (see number 3) is that it basically takes care of this one. If you start by investing as much as you must to reach your goal, you can take what's left over and do whatever you want with it. By making saving a priority, you can't spend more than you can afford to. The important thing is that you spend way less than you make. To reiterate: spend way less than you make.

7. The rich make short-term sacrifices

Think bigger than right now. Think about the future effect your decisions will have on your life. The whole point of getting wealthy is to have more of what you want. But sometimes you have to trade off what you want now for more of that or something better later. Think bigger than what you want right now.

8. The Rich get help.

Know what you are good at and leave the money management to a professional. Focus on the unique value you bring to the world to make money to invest. Don't be completely clueless about managing money either. Understand the basics at least well enough to know what your financial advisor is telling you. The information is cheap and easy to get. Rich people have written lots of books about it.

Millionaire entrepreneur, Vladimir Gendelman says,

I know how to build and grow businesses, but I leave my money management to a professional financial advisor.

9. The wealthy do math.

We're not talking about trigonometry and advanced polynomials; just simple addition, subtraction, multiplication and division — third grade stuff. Wealthy people run the numbers when they make a decision. For example, poor people believe that when a car begins to have problems, it's better to get a newer car so they don't have to spend as much for maintenance and repairs. This is not necessarily true. You can spend thousands of dollars a year repairing a car and be financially way ahead when compared to buying a car. Think about all the expense of a car purchase. Do the math.

10. The wealthy take advantage of opportunity.

Rich people know that things like IRA's and 401k's are tax-free or tax-deferred growth and they take full advantage of them. When an opportunity like that arises, take advantage of it. If you also do the math (number 9), you'll see exactly how beneficial this is.

Managing money like the wealthy is learnable and it's not hard. If you want to be rich, manage your money using these 10 principles and you'll be on your way. You'll have to make some sacrifices in the short-term, learn some stuff and work hard to earn the money you invest. The result is a really cool tool that lets you do a lot of good in the world and have a blast doing it, which is all anybody really wants. If you can't handle all ten, just remember this: spend less than you make.

So you see my dear friends, making money or being rich, is not some rocket science. It is totally about what you know and what you don't know. If you do not know how to manage your money properly, it does not matter how much you earn, you will still be broke. So the key point when it comes to being rich and staying wealthy is not just about making more money. Even though that is a very vital part of it, but the major key needed is managing money.

The problem the middle class have is not the inability to make more money but rather the inability to manage and channel their money properly. It is therefore an effort in futility to struggle and work so hard just because you want to make more money but without self-educating yourself on financial management. Without a proper management skill, your money will leave just the way it came. It will develop wings and fly away.

So add to your hard work wisdom, in this case wisdom in the area of money management and the laws/ principles of money; if you want to be rich. But if you are comfortable with running the rat race, living from pay check to pay check, then you do not need this wisdom. But if you really want to make a difference in life, you are welcome to a world of a whole new possibility lying before you.

What you should have in mind is that riches do not just appear in one day, neither do people get rich automatically. It takes persistence, consistency and perseverance. It is a progressive process. It has to be a habit not just an act you carry out occasionally. Those ten ways of managing money should be what you do on a daily basis and be committed to it. Sooner or later you will be amazed at the amount of wealth at your disposal if you will be patient and diligent to follow through these rules.

Now that you know what the rich know; it's time to put it into practice. The beginnings when you take your baby steps are not always the easiest of time but you have to take those steps anyway. Until you learn to step out of your comfort zone, you will not be able to step into your destiny. The ball is now in your court, whether you take actions or you remain dormant and reluctant, the choice is the still yours to make.

Will you choose a temporary pain in order to have Permanent riches or will you choose temporary comfort and live in permanent pain as a slave to your pay check and salary? Choose wisely!!!

GOLDEN NUGGETS

1. The rich invest and multiply money

2. Don't confuse needs with wants

3. The wealthy forget about instant gratification

4. The wealthy understand the difference between wants and needs.

5. The rich know and understand that money is not meant for spending.

6. Making more money without management ability will still lead to poverty.

7. Without a proper management skill, your money will leave just the way it came.

8. A Penny Saved Is A Penny Earned

9. Think about the future effect your money decisions today will have on your life.

10. You'll have to make some sacrifices in the short-term, to get the desired result you need in the long run.

11. Decide what you want your life to be like, figure out how much that will cost and do exactly what you need to do to get there.

12. The wealthy take advantage of opportunity.

CHAPTER 24
SAVING ALONE CANNOT MAKE YOU RICH (INFLATION)

This is one major fact the rich, people with abundance mindset know that the poor, people with poverty mind-set are ignorant of. Saving alone can never make anyone rich. It is a secret the rich know and live by. You cannot save your way to riches or wealth. Your number one goal for saving should not be for the purpose of getting rich but for investment. It is then your investment that makes you rich.

The old jargon of saving for retirement in order to live in financial freedom when you retire, that is a myth. The greatest self-deception you could ever think of. Saving all your working days for retirement without investing your money is preparing yourself for a life time of poverty and lack in your old age. You have to begin to throw away this useless advice and approach that have made slaves of many more than empower them.

The rich know that their money should not just sit in a savings account in a bank or lying dormant without being in active service to them. The rich know that their money should be at work for them. So they put their money to work. That is why they do not work for money and live in financial freedom. It is not those who save the most that become financially free but those who have taken a step further to put their saved money to work. As important as saving maybe, saving alone will not make you rich. It is only the first step to financial freedom

All the 'get rich' advice in the world revolves around saving your money. Here's a tough pill to swallow, but you won't get rich by saving your money alone. You can't get rich by going without Starbuck's coffees.

The only way you will ever get rich is by creating a product, being a producer, and making massive sales and sky-rocketing your income. You don't get rich by having a limited income and saving a portion of that limited income. That's the silly little fib that has been sold to you.

Saving money is reactive. You don't get rich by reaction, you get rich by pro-action. You have to be a producer to get rich. A money saver is a reducer. They reduce the amount of Starbuck's coffees they consume to save some money, they reduce this and reduce that but what they don't usually do is reduce the big expenses and what they never do is produce. You cannot get rich by reducing, you cannot get rich by saving, you cannot get rich from a 401(k).

The way you get rich is by increasing your earnings, not by saving from your capped and limited post-tax earnings from a job. The money saver thinking he will retire rich is a dreamer. The money maker is the doer.

I see people, expats, who worked their whole lives and now either live on a pension or live on savings. The men who live on pensions don't have enough money, to almost any man they complain of high costs of things, usually food products. They live in a 3rd world country and can hardly afford the basic necessities of life.

The other ones, the savers, usually have a different sob story to tell. The story of running out of money. They saved up their whole life to retire like a king but, whoops, they ran out of money. The money saving dreamers simply choose to ignore the reality of inflation. A dollar to-day will not be worth a dollar in 5 to 10 year's time talk more of longer years.

The key to wealth is to make more money by owning income producing businesses and assets, not by saving a portion of a limited income from a limited paycheck. They used to tell me the key to wealth was to work a "good job", save your money and open up a 401(k). I was told this by non-rich family friends, teachers, personal bankers etc. people that are not rich themselves. If these people actually knew how to get rich they wouldn't be working the un-skilled jobs they work. They wouldn't be working jobs at all. These are people working jobs that anyone with a college degree in any field can work. They make about 50k per year, about 30k after taxes and yet they are the ones that advice or tell other people how to achieve success.

I used to have a friend who told me that one of his family members that tells him all the time "get a good job, especially in I.T., open a 401(k) and you'll be rich when you retire". In his words: Like many young men I was aimless at that age, but I wasn't stupid. I could see very clearly he was living beyond his means. I did not see him for a number of years. I met him again after his house was foreclosed by the bank because he could not make the payments. I went to his new house, which was rented to him by another family member, and what I saw shocked me: two new leased cars in the driveway. This was a self-proclaimed money expert. This was a man who had the gall to speak about becoming wealthy, and this type of man is the average person giving you money advice.

The people who preach this type of "save your money, get a job, open a 401(k)" baloney are people working unskilled and highly unsatisfying jobs and they are living from paycheck to paycheck. They don't provide value and they work worthless jobs and they often withdraw money from their own get rich slow schemes, the 401(k). They are highly unmotivated people and their advice should be ignored completely. Anyone with a garbage diploma in any garbage field can do what they do.

If it worked as they say it does then they wouldn't be living from hand to mouth, complaining about bills all the time. They wouldn't be working at jobs, they would be developing businesses and making SALES and increasing earnings, not putting 10% of your paycheck into a savings account or 401(k) and leave it alone hoping or believing that it will develop into billions.

I want you to know this, you will not get rich by saving your money but you will go broke by spending all of your money. So you do in fact need to save your money. Not for retirement, but for opportunity. You've heard the phrase spend money to make money. If you want to make big money you will eventually have to make a big investment. If you have bills up to your eyeballs you'll never be able to focus on making real money because you'll be working some job to pay off your debts.

Stay out of debt, don't be a money waster, educate yourself, spend time on developing income producing goods = the key to wealth. If you must go into debt, or borrow money, let it be for the purpose of multiplying money, i.e investment. Never borrow to eat or spend. Also remember that when you "invest" in a 401(k) you leave your future in the hands of the unqualified. Who cares more about your future, you or an anonymous money manager playing a game with your savings? Leaving your future in the hands of the unqualified is stupid.

When you make stupid decisions with your money don't be surprised when it comes back to bite you in the behind. When it all crashes down, and you break your crown you can point your finger but there's no one around. That last sentence is a quote from a famous song by the most successful heavy metal band of all time, Metallica, and it's a quote I often think of when I hear elders complain about money. They had their whole lives to build real wealth. They wasted it and threw it all away and point their finger when they don't have enough money. You and you alone have to keep a keen eye on your assets, you and you alone can provide for your future. You are responsible for you, give up responsibility and you have no right to complain when it doesn't work out for you.

A few simple rules to live by:

Trust no one – Unless you are someone's loving and devoted wife or mother no one gives a damn about your future. Least of all 'money managers'. Point the finger inward, never outward. It's your job and your responsibility to make sure you have a future. It pays to be paranoid. Verify everything.

Produce income – Wealth isn't coming to you via a paycheck and $3 saved daily on a cup of coffee. It is coming from production, from action, from earning more money.

Live below your means – You simply cannot be in debt lest you want to work in a 9-5 job forever. Debt is slavery, money and time is freedom. Think big to live little. Cut down the big expenses like housing, automobile, higher education, credit card debt, cell phone bill etc. When your biggest bills are tiny you can afford all the little coffee's you want. Big expenses do not increase quality of life, they increase stress. No bills, no stress. Take action when opportunity presents itself – The real reason to save money, is to use it to make more money.

The joke: To get rich, save your money from your limited income stream and be rich in 40 or 50 years. The reality: To get rich make a lot more money now. You can live like a king in the near future, or you can pretend you'll live like a king in 40 years, but don't be too surprised if it all crashes down and you break your crown and you point your finger but there's no one around.

If you've always wondered what the steps were to becoming rich, it's actually quite simple. In fact, you might already know them. The trouble is… even though you know them; you might not actually do it. It is one thing to know, it is another thing to apply your knowledge in your day to day life. I will therefore like to call on you to put the knowledge you get from this book into action. That is the only way you can get positive result.

So what are the 3 steps?

- Earn income

- Spend less than you earn

- Invest

That's basically it. I told you that you might already know the three steps. So do you actually practice them? A lot of times people think that the key to getting rich is to simply earn a LOT more money. "If only I had an extra $1,000 a month." It's very easy to think that just by making or having more money, all our financial worries will disappear. But that's not true. And the reason is because for most people out there, making more money simply gives an excuse to start spending more — it's called lifestyle inflation.

Have you ever got a $500 raise only to start blowing your extra hard-earned money on new clothes, bags, watches, restaurants, and entertainment? Not only that, you justify your spending by telling yourself you deserve it. Because you've worked so hard and "I should be allowed to indulge myself". Now don't get me wrong. It's perfectly fine to reward yourself when you receive a nice raise or achieve a financial goal. But if you increase your spending every single month to "reward yourself" then you're back to square one. You're making more money but you're not any richer.

You see, even if you make twenty thousand dollars a month but you spend twenty thousand dollars every month, you're still BROKE. It doesn't take a math genius to know that you need to spend less than you earn in order to grow richer. But Spending Less to Save is Not Enough. The reason is quite simple — inflation.

As inflation rises, the amount of goods/services you can buy with the same dollar decreases. The average rate of inflation in some countries is about 4% a year. That might not seem like much but in 30 years; every dollar you save now will only be worth thirty cents. That's why saving alone will not make you richer; every year that inflation rises, you get poorer! This is the very reason why you need to invest your money. So you can retain its value and as well multiply it. Which is why the final step – invest – is probably the most important step of all.

5 REASONS WHY INVESTING IS SO IMPORTANT

We all hear that investing is important but here's exactly why:

1. **Your income is limited if you do not invest.**

As a worker whose income is tied to the number of hours you work, the only way to make more money is to spend more time working for it. But no matter how hard or long you want to work, there's a cap to how many hours you can work in a day. Pretty soon you'll hit a physical limit that no one can overcome: There are 24 hours in a day and for most people they need at least half of it to sleep, spend time with their family, eat, recuperate etc.

2. **Investing gives you potentially unlimited, passive income**

Unlike being tied to a job that makes you trade a finite resource, time, for money, investing gives you the ability to make unlimited passive income. The more you invest successfully, the more wealth and income you'll make. There's virtually no limit to how much you can make. And because it's your money (instead of you) working for it, your investments will generate passive income for you whether you're enjoying a holiday, sleeping or watching viral cat videos on YouTube.

3. **You can't work forever, you know**

As young, hot and virile as you think you are right now, there will come a time when you look as attractive as a bucket of smashed crabs and you can't physically work anymore. If you didn't invest, the moment you stop working is the moment you stop making money. In other words, you need your investments to provide you with passive income to fund your living expenses when you retire.

4. Invest with inflation

Rather than let inflation eat away at your wealth as a saver, why not let inflation help you as an investor? As prices of goods and services rise year after year, so do the sales and profits of the biggest companies in the world and in turn their stock prices. That's why the stock market index always rises in an inflationary environment in the long run.

5. Compound interest

This is probably the most common reason you hear about why you must invest. Compound interest is basically "interest on interest". Did you know that if you just set aside a hundred dollars a month and invested it at 20% per annum, you'll have $1.38 million in your pocket in thirty years? Does that surprise you? That's the power of compound interest and why even just saving one hundred dollars a month can make such a huge difference in the long run.

IMPORTANT FACTORS FOR YOUR IN-VESTMENT SUCCESS

If you're new to investing, it's pretty easy to feel overwhelmed. There are strange words to figure out, complicated ideas to understand, new decisions to make, and plenty of conflicting advice about all of it. It's almost enough to make you want to avoid the topic altogether. But here's the truth: It doesn't take a Ph.D. in finance to be a good investor. In fact, the most important investment decisions you have to make are actually pretty simple.

So here are the five most important factors for your investment success:

1. Your Savings Rate

The amount you save is far and away the most important factor as you start investing. Nothing else comes close. You'll hear plenty of people talk about ways they think you can get better returns. As important as that might sound, the level of investment and returns you have is directly proportional to the amount of money you have been able to save to invest.

So how much should you save? I personally believe that you should start your savings if you are just beginning with at least 10 percent of your income and when you are comfortable at that stage, you increase it to 20 percent, then to 30 percent, then to 40 and 50 percent. Depending on how disciplined and purposeful you are. It also depends to a large extent on how much you earn.

So check out what works for you and stick to it. Some people can even save up to 70 percent of their income and live on only 30 percent. But like I said, it is different for every individual, work out the amount you can save without having problems with meeting your fundamental daily needs. Small changes in your lifestyle and expenses can really add up over time. However you do it, focus first and foremost on the amount you save. No other factor will have as big of an impact.

2. What You Invest In

Asset allocation is the fancy term for how you decide to divvy up your money among different types of investments. And this is an important decision, since the research suggests that 90% of the investment return you receive is dependent on the kinds of things you invest in, rather than the specific investment choices you make. In other words, deciding to invest in the stock market will have a big impact on your returns. But the specific stocks you pick matter a lot less. And at the highest level, your main decision will be how to split your money between stocks and bonds.

Stocks represent ownership in a company. They offer the highest potential return, but also the highest risk of loss. Stocks are typically a good place to invest some of your long-term money, but are riskier when dealing with shorter-term goals. Bonds are actually loans you give to companies. Just like a loan you would take out personally, they pay an interest rate and over time the entire loan is paid back. They don't offer as much return as stocks, but they also carry less risk.

Your big decision is essentially how much of your money to put toward each. The more you put toward stocks, the higher your potential return, but the higher your potential loss as well, especially in the short term. A good rule of thumb is to be comfortable losing half the money you have in stocks in any given year without changing your plan. So if you have 60% of your money in stocks, you should expect to face about a 30% loss in your investments at some point in your life (though it may bounce back over time).

3. How You Diversify

Diversification is another fancy word that investment people like to throw around. But all it really means is investing your money in a lot of different things instead of putting all your eggs in one basket. And diversification is important because it's the only way to decrease your investment risk without decreasing your expected return. In other words, diversification is pretty darn cool!

One way to diversify is with your asset allocation. Putting some money into stocks and some into bonds means you're diversified across different types of investments. You could even go a little further by splitting those into U.S. stocks and international stocks, and U.S. bonds and international bonds, just to make sure you have everything covered.

But you can also diversify within those major categories. For example, instead of picking just a few U.S. stocks to invest in, you could pick an index fund that invests in the entire U.S. stock market. When you own a little bit of every company in America, no single company can send your investments into the tank. This kind of simple diversification has the benefit of decreasing your risk of loss without decreasing the return you expect to receive.

4. What You Pay

With most things in life, you can expect that higher quality comes at a higher price. Not so with investing. As Vanguard founder John Bogle once said: "In investing, you get what you don't pay for." It turns out that one of the best ways to increase your returns is to lower your costs. In fact, the investment research company Moringstar found that cost is the single best predictor of a mutual fund's future return, even better than its own star rating system!

The less money you pay for the privilege of investing, the more you have available to invest in your future. Watch fees like a hawk and watch your returns improve.

5. Sticking to Your Plan

Lethargy bordering on sloth remains the cornerstone of our investment style. (Warren Buffett)

There will be many times where you're tempted to change your investment strategy. When the market is up, you may want to be more aggressive. When the market is down, you may want to get out. When your co-worker is bragging about the stock he just bought, you may be tempted to buy it, too.

Many investors give in to those temptations and end up with returns that lag the market as a whole. They end up buying high and selling low, just the opposite of what you want to do. To avoid that, you'll have to tune out the noise and keep doing what you set out to do, no matter what kind of craziness is happening all around you. Stick to your contributions. Stick to your investment choices. Don't let the news of the day change your mind. It's not easy, but that consistency will keep you on track through the ups and downs.

TEN THINGS TO CONSIDER BEFORE YOU MAKE INVESTING DECISIONS

Given recent market events, you may be wondering whether you should make changes to your investment portfolio. The SEC's Office of Investor Education and Advocacy is concerned that some investors, including bargain hunters and mattress stuffers, are making rapid investment decisions without considering their long-term financial goals. Before you make any decision, consider these areas of importance:

209

1. **Draw a personal financial roadmap.**

Before you make any investing decision, sit down and take an honest look at your entire financial situation -- especially if you've never made a financial plan before.

The first step to successful investing is figuring out your goals and risk tolerance – either on your own or with the help of a financial professional. There is no guarantee that you'll make money from your investments. But if you get the facts about saving and investing and follow through with an intelligent plan, you should be able to gain financial security over the years and enjoy the benefits of managing your money.

2. **Evaluate your comfort zone in taking on risk.**

All investments involve some degree of risk. If you intend to purchase securities - such as stocks, bonds, or mutual funds - it's important that you understand before you invest that you could lose some or all of your money. Unlike deposits at FDIC-insured banks and NCUA-insured credit unions, the money you invest in securities typically is not federally insured. You could lose your principal, which is the amount you've invested. That's true even if you purchase your investments through a bank.

The reward for taking on risk is the potential for a greater investment return. If you have a financial goal with a long time horizon, you are likely to make more money by carefully investing in asset categories with greater risk, like stocks or bonds, rather than restricting your investments to assets with less risk, like cash equivalents. On the other hand, investing solely in cash investments may be appropriate for short-term financial goals. The principal concern for individuals investing in cash equivalents is inflation risk, which is the risk that inflation will outpace and erode returns over time.

3. Consider an appropriate mix of investments.

By including asset categories with investment returns that move up and down under different market conditions within a portfolio, an investor can help protect against significant losses. Historically, the returns of the three major asset categories – stocks, bonds, and cash – have not moved up and down at the same time. Market conditions that cause one asset category to do well often cause another asset category to have average or poor returns. By investing in more than one asset category, you'll reduce the risk that you'll lose money and your portfolio's overall investment returns will have a smoother ride. If one asset category's investment return falls, you'll be in a position to counteract your losses in that asset category with better investment returns in another asset category.

In addition, asset allocation is important because it has major impact on whether you will meet your financial goal. If you don't include enough risk in your portfolio, your investments may not earn a large enough return to meet your goal. For example, if you are saving for a long-term goal, such as retirement or college, most financial experts agree that you will likely need to include at least some stock or stock mutual funds in your portfolio.

Life-cycle Funds - To accommodate investors who prefer to use one investment to save for a particular investment goal, such as retirement, some mutual fund companies have begun offering a product known as a "life-cycle fund." A life-cycle fund is a diversified mutual fund that automatically shifts towards a more conservative mix of investments as it approaches a particular year in the future, known as its "target date" A life-cycle fund investor picks a fund with the right target date based on his or her particular investment goal. The managers of the fund then make all decisions about asset allocation, diversification, and rebalancing. It's easy to identify a lifecycle fund because its name will likely refer to its target date. For example, you might see life-cycle funds with names like "Portfolio 2015," "Retirement Fund 2030," or "Target 2045."

4. **Be careful if investing heavily in shares of employer's stock or any individual stock.**

One of the most important ways to lessen the risks of investing is to diversify your investments. It's common sense: don't put all your eggs in one basket. By picking the right group of investments within an asset category, you may be able to limit your losses and reduce the fluctuations of investment returns without sacrificing too much potential gain.

You'll be exposed to significant investment risk if you invest heavily in shares of your employer's stock or any individual stock. If that stock does poorly or the company goes bankrupt, you'll probably lose a lot of money (and perhaps your job).

5. **Create and maintain an emergency fund.**

Most smart investors put enough money in a savings product to cover an emergency, like sudden unemployment. Some make sure they have up to six months of their income in savings so that they know it will absolutely be there for them when they need it.

6. **Pay off high interest credit card debt.**

There is no investment strategy anywhere that pays off as well as, or with less risk than, merely paying off all high interest debt you may have. If you owe money on high interest credit cards, the wisest thing you can do under any market conditions is to pay off the balance in full as quickly as possible.

7. **Consider dollar cost averaging.**

Through the investment strategy known as "dollar cost averaging," you can protect yourself from the risk of investing all of your money at the wrong time by following a consistent pattern of adding new money to your investment over a long period of time. By making regular investments with the same amount of money each time, you will buy more of an investment when its price is low and less of the investment when its price is high. Individuals that typically make a lump-sum contribution to an individual retirement account either at the end of the calendar year or in early April may want to consider "dollar cost averaging" as an investment strategy, especially in a volatile market.

8. **Take advantage of "free money" from employer.**

In many employer-sponsored retirement plans, the employer will match some or all of your contributions. If your employer offers a retirement plan and you do not contribute enough to get your employer's maximum match, you are passing up "free money" for your retirement savings.

Keep Your Money Working - In most cases, a workplace plan is the most effective way to save for retirement. Consider your options carefully before borrowing from your retirement plan. In particular, avoid using a 401(k) debit card, except as a last resort. Money you borrow now will reduce the savings available to grow over the years and ultimately what you have when you retire. Also, if you don't repay the loan, you may pay federal income taxes and penalties.

9. Consider rebalancing portfolio occasionally.

Rebalancing is bringing your portfolio back to your original asset allocation mix. By rebalancing, you'll ensure that your portfolio does not overemphasize one or more asset categories, and you'll return your portfolio to a comfortable level of risk. Stick with Your Plan: Buy Low, Sell High - Shifting money away from an asset category when it is doing well in favor of an asset category that is doing poorly may not be easy, but it can be a wise move. By cutting back on the current "winners" and adding more of the current so-called "losers," rebalancing forces you to buy low and sell high.

You can rebalance your portfolio based either on the calendar or on your investments. Many financial experts recommend that investors rebalance their portfolios on a regular time interval, such as every six or twelve months. The advantage of this method is that the calendar is a reminder of when you should consider rebalancing. Others recommend rebalancing only when the relative weight of an asset class increases or decreases more than a certain percentage that you've identified in advance. The advantage of this method is that your investments tell you when to rebalance. In either case, rebalancing tends to work best when done on a relatively infrequent basis.

10. Avoid circumstances that can lead to fraud.

Scam artists read the headlines, too. Often, they'll use a highly publicized news item to lure potential investors and make their "opportunity" sound more legitimate. The SEC recommends that you ask questions and check out the answers with an unbiased source before you invest. Always take your time and talk to trusted friends and family members before investing.

GOLDEN NUGGETS

1. Saving alone will not make you rich
2. One of the most important ways to lessen the risks of investing is to diversify your investments.
3. Investing gives you potentially unlimited, passive income
4. Draw a personal financial roadmap.
5. The reward for taking on risk is the potential for a greater investment return.
6. Make it a priority to live below your means.
7. Keep Your Money Working
8. Never borrow to eat or spend.
9. The more you invest successfully, the more wealth and income you'll make.
10. Only invest in what you know
11. Take advantage of "free money" from employer.
12. All investments involve some degree of risk

CHAPTER 25

ENVIRONMENT MATTERS (THE RICH SURROUND THEMSELVES WITH THE RICH)

If you have not known the importance or effects of your environment on you, then I will advise you do yourself a favor by doing that analysis. It is a popular saying that you will remain the same way you are in the next ten years to come, except for the people you meet and the books you read.

This is something the rich know and take great advantage of. The rich know that association matters. Iron they say sharpens iron. If you therefore want to be rich, you might want to ask yourself this sincere question, who are my friends? What kind of associations do I keep? What is my environment like? What kind of books do I read?

If you give yourself a sincere answer to these questions, then you will know which part of the spectrum you are heading towards. If all your friends are poorer than you are with little or no financial knowledge, I bet you definitely know where you are tilting to. If you have never read books on finance, investing, wealth creation, I also bet by now you know the answer to which of the parts you are tilting to.

The best thing you can do for yourself if you want to be rich is to begin to put your associations and friends in check. What kind of environment have you built for yourself? How knowledgeable are you on the topic of finance? How many books have you read in the past year on finance, investment, entrepreneurship, etc.? Don't ever forget that old saying, show me your friends and I will tell you who you are.

The simple reason why the rich surround themselves with the rich is because the rich think differently. In order to have people of like minds around them, they surround themselves with the rich. It is obvious that the view of life of the rich is totally different from the view point of the poor. Let us take a look at the 21 ways the rich think differently by Steve Siebold:

1. Average people think MONEY is the root of all evil. Rich people believe POVERTY is the root of all evil. "The average person has been brainwashed to believe rich people are lucky or dishonest," That's why there's a certain shame that comes along with "getting rich" in lower-income communities. "The world class knows that while having money doesn't guarantee happiness, it does make your life easier and more enjoyable."

2. Average people think selfishness is a vice. Rich people think selfishness is a virtue. "The rich go out there and try to make themselves happy. They don't try to pretend to save the world," Siebold told Business Insider. The problem is that middle class people see that as a negative - and it's keeping them poor, he writes. "If you're not taking care of you, you're not in a position to help anyone else. You can't give what you don't have."

3. Average people have a lottery mentality. Rich people have an action mentality. "While the

masses are waiting to pick the right numbers and praying for prosperity, the great ones are solving problems," Siebold writes. "The hero [middle class people] are waiting for may be God, government, their boss or their spouse. It's the average person's level of thinking that breeds this approach to life and living while the clock keeps ticking away."

4. Average people think the road to riches is paved with formal education. Rich people believe in acquiring specific knowledge. "Many world-class performers have little formal education, and have amassed their wealth through the acquisition and subsequent sale of specific knowledge," he writes. "Meanwhile, the masses are convinced that master's degrees and doctorates are the way to wealth, mostly because they are trapped in the linear line of thought that holds them back from higher levels of consciousness...The wealthy aren't interested in the means, only the end."

5. Average people long for the good old days. Rich people dream of the future. "Self-made millionaires get rich because they're willing to bet on themselves and project their dreams, goals and ideas into an unknown future," Siebold writes. "People who believe their best days are behind them rarely get rich, and often struggle with unhappiness and depression."

6. Average people see money through the eyes of emotion. Rich people think about money logically. "An ordinarily smart, well-educated and otherwise successful person can be instantly

transformed into a fear-based, scarcity driven thinker whose greatest financial aspiration is to retire comfortably," he writes. "The world class sees money for what it is and what it's not, through the eyes of logic. The great ones know money is a critical tool that presents options and opportunities."

7. Average people earn money doing things they don't love. Rich people follow their passion. "To the average person, it looks like the rich are working all the time," Siebold says. "But one of the smartest strategies of the world class is doing what they love and finding a way to get paid for it." On the other hand, middle class take jobs they don't enjoy "because they need the money and they've been trained in school and conditioned by society to live in a linear thinking world that equates earning money with physical or mental effort."

8. Average people set low expectations so they're never disappointed. Rich people are up for the challenge. "Psychologists and other mental health experts often advise people to set low expectations for their life to ensure they are not disappointed," Siebold writes. "No one would ever strike it rich and live their dreams without huge expectations."

9. Average people believe you have to DO something to get rich. Rich people believe you have to BE something to get rich. "That's why people like Donald Trump go from millionaire to nine billion dollars in debt and come back richer than

ever," he writes. "While the masses are fixated on the doing and the immediate results of their actions, the great ones are learning and growing from every experience, whether it's a success or a failure, knowing their true reward is becoming a human success machine that eventually produces outstanding results."

10. Average people believe you need money to make money. Rich people use other people's money. Linear thought might tell people to make money in order to earn more, but Siebold says the rich aren't afraid to fund their future from other people's pockets. "Rich people know not being solvent enough to personally afford something is not relevant. The real question is, 'Is this worth buying, investing in, or pursuing?'" he writes.

11. Average people believe the markets are driven by logic and strategy. Rich people know they're driven by emotion and greed. Investing successfully in the stock market isn't just about a fancy math formula. "The rich know that the primary emotions that drive financial markets are fear and greed, and they factor this into all trades and trends they observe," Siebold writes. "This knowledge of human nature and its overlapping impact on trading give them strategic advantage in building greater wealth through leverage."

12. Average people live beyond their means. Rich people live below theirs. "Here's how to live below your means and tap into the secret wealthy people have used for centuries: Get rich so you

can afford to," he writes. "The rich live below their means, not because they're so savvy, but because they make so much money that they can afford to live like royalty while still having a king's ransom socked away for the future."

13. Average people teach their children how to survive. Rich people teach their kids to get rich. Rich parents teach their kids from an early age about the world of "haves" and "have-nots," Siebold says. Even he admits many people have argued that he's supporting the idea of elitism. "[People] say parents are teaching their kids to look down on the masses because they're poor. This isn't true," he writes. "What they're teaching their kids is to see the world through the eyes of objective reality-the way society really is." If children understand wealth early on, they'll be more likely to strive for it later in life.

14. Average people let money stress them out. Rich people find peace of mind in wealth. The reason wealthy people earn more wealth is that they're not afraid to admit that money can solve most problems, Siebold says. "[The middle class] sees money as a never-ending necessary evil that must be endured as part of life. The world class see money as the great liberator, and with enough of it, they are able to purchase financial peace of mind."

15. Average people would rather be entertained than educated. Rich people would rather be educated than entertained. While the rich don't put much stock in furthering wealth through formal

education, they appreciate the power of learning long after college is over, Siebold says. "Walk into a wealthy person's home and one of the first things you'll see is an extensive library of books they've used to educate themselves on how to become more successful," he writes. "The middle class reads novels, tabloids and entertainment magazines."

16. Average people think rich people are snobs. Rich people just want to surround themselves with like-minded people. The negative money mentality poisoning the middle class is what keeps the rich hanging out with the rich, he says. "[Rich people] can't afford the messages of doom and gloom," he writes. "This is often misinterpreted by the masses as snobbery. Labeling the world class as snobs is another way the middle class finds to feel better about themselves and their chosen path of mediocrity."

17. Average people focus on saving. Rich people focus on earning. Siebold theorizes that the wealthy focus on what they'll gain by taking risks, rather than how to save what they have. "The masses are so focused on clipping coupons and living frugally they miss major opportunities," he writes. "Even in the midst of a cash flow crisis, the rich reject the nickel and dime thinking of the masses. They are the masters of focusing their mental energy where it belongs: on the big money."

18. Average people play it safe with money. Rich people know when to take risks. "Leverage is the

watchword of the rich," Siebold writes. "Every investor loses money on occasion, but the world class know no matter what happens, they will always be able to earn more."

19. Average people love to be comfortable. Rich people find comfort in uncertainty. For the most part, it takes guts to take the risks necessary to make it as a millionaire, a challenge most middle class thinkers aren't comfortable living with. "Physical, psychological, and emotional comfort is the primary goal of the middle class mindset," Siebold writes. World class thinkers learn early on that becoming a millionaire isn't easy and the need for comfort can be devastating. They learn to be comfortable while operating in a state of ongoing uncertainty."

20. Average people never make the connection between money and health. Rich people know money can save your life. While the middle class squabble over the virtues of Obamacare and their company's health plan, the super wealthy are enrolled in a super elite "boutique medical care" association, Siebold says. "They pay a substantial yearly membership fee that guarantees them 24-hour access to a private physician who only serves a small group of members," he writes. "Some wealthy neighborhoods have implemented this strategy and even require the physician to live in the neighborhood."

21. Average people believe they must choose between a great family and being rich. Rich people know you can have it all. The idea the wealth must

come at the expense of family time is nothing but a "cop-out", Siebold says. "The masses have been brainwashed to believe it's an either/or equation," he writes. "The rich know you can have anything you want if you approach the challenge with a mindset rooted in love and abundance."

Now that we have taken a close look at the way the rich think differently from the poor and the middle class, do you think there is a need for you to seek to associate with the rich in order to begin to see life from the perspective they have seen life from that have result to riches? I guess the answer is yes. If you truly want to be rich and live in financial freedom, then you have to take the bold step of changing your environment by changing your association.

You cannot expect to have a different result, if you keep on repeating the same thing you have been doing over and over again. It is high time you stepped out of your comfort zone. Get yourself into the company of the rich and ask them constructive questions that can help you in your pursuit of financial freedom. This is the time for action. It is either you do it now or you will never do it. Don't procrastinate, act now! First of all work on changing your mindset about money. Change your associations. Invest in yourself. Buy good financial empowering books to read. Make friends with the rich and ask them constructive questions. Be a good student and watch yourself move from poverty to riches. Welcome to the World of Abundance!

"1. Rich people believe "I create my life." Poor people believe "Life happens to me."

2. Rich people play the money game to win. Poor people play the money game to not lose.

3. Rich people are committed to being rich. Poor people want to be rich.

4. Rich people think big. Poor people think small.

5. Rich people focus on opportunities. Poor people focus on obstacles.

6. Rich people admire other rich and successful people. Poor people resent rich and successful people.

7. Rich people associate with positive, successful people. Poor people associate with negative or unsuccessful people.

8. Rich people are willing to promote themselves and their values. Poor people think negatively about selling and promotion.

9. Rich people are bigger than their problems. Poor people are smaller than their problems.

10. Rich people are excellent receivers. Poor people are poor receivers.

11. Rich people choose to get paid based on re-

sults. Poor people choose to get paid based on time.

12. Rich people think "both". Poor people think "either/or".

13. Rich people focus on their net worth. Poor people focus on their working income.

14. Rich people manage their money well. Poor people mismanage their money.

15. Rich people have their money work hard for them. Poor people work hard for their money.

16. Rich people act in spite of fear. Poor people let fear stop them.

17. Rich people constantly learn and grow. Poor people think they already know."

T. Harv Eker

GOLDEN NUGGETS

1. Your environment matters

2. If you want to be rich then surround yourself with the rich

3. The simple reason why the rich surround themselves with the rich is because the rich think differently.

4. Rich people are committed to being rich. Poor people want to be rich.

5. Make friends with the rich and ask them constructive questions.

6. Average people love to be comfortable. Rich people find comfort in uncertainty.

7. Rich people focus on opportunities. Poor people focus on obstacles.

8. Average people play it safe with money. Rich people know when to take risks.

9. Average people would rather be entertained than educated.

10. Rich people would rather be educated than entertained.

11. You cannot expect to have a different result, if you keep on repeating the same thing you have been doing over and over again.

12. It is high time you stepped out of your comfort zone.

CONCLUSION

Having gone through this book, Poverty Mindset VS Abundance Mindset, I believe you now understand that living in financial freedom is not a rocket science but rather the knowledge and application of financial principles. You also know the reason why some people live in poverty irrespective of how hard they work, and others live in abundance. It is now clear to you that hard work is not enough to get you into financial freedom. Beyond working very hard, there are important financial keys and principles to live by in order to live in financial freedom.

The knowledge you got from this book, if applied will enable you to live free from being under the bondage of working for money all your life. With the principles in this book you will be able to put your money to work for you.

I believe you now understand that poverty or riches is not dependent on your country of birth or your country of residence, but rather on the state of your mind, totally dependent on the principles of money you know and are in operation in your life. It is therefore not enough to know, but you must apply to see the result you desire.

I would like to say a big congratulation to you! Because you now have the keys and principles you need to riches and living   a life of financial freedom. You don't need to run about any more looking for countries to go to for greener pastures. Especially, to my Nigerian country men and Africans at large.

I am glad because with the application of the golden principles documented in this book, I can see Nigerians and Africans at large moving from a country and continent known for poverty and lack to a place of riches and abundance, not only in Africa, but all developing countries around the world, and individuals struggling with poverty and lack.

Dear friend, the ball is now in your court. Go therefore and make your desire to living your life in financial freedom a reality by applying the principles you have learnt from this book. Remember, you cannot live in financial freedom without obeying financial laws and practicing the financial principles.

I therefore welcome you to living financially free, the life you so much desired! Good luck!!

INFORMATION ABOUT THE EMBASSY OF GOD CHURCH AND PASTOR SUNDAY ADELAJA

Pastor Sunday Adelaja — The only black man in the world that leads a congregation of mostly Caucasians in 50 countries. Below are some facts about Pastor Sunday's life and ministry.

- Pastor Sunday is the pastor of the largest Evangelical Church in Europe with a population of 99,9% white Europeans in Kiev Ukraine.
- His ministry has charity units that feed over 5000 people on a daily basis.
- Through his ministry over 30 thousand people have been delivered from drug and alcohol addictions.
- He helped raise over 200 millionaires in US dollars in his church, most of whom were former drug/ alcohol addicts and societal outcasts.
- He has raised a global movement that is influencing over 70million people around the globe.
- Branches of his church are in over 50 countries.
- He has spoken in different nations of the world on National Transformation.
- Pastor Sunday is one of the few, if not the only African, who has ever spoken in the US senate.
- Pastor Sunday is one of the few African pastors who has spoken on the floor of the UN.
- He has addressed the Japanese Members of parliament.
- He has spoken in the Knesset to members of Israeli parliament. The list goes on and on.
- His ministry has over 500 hundred government officials holding different government positions in Ukraine.
- He has written and published over 300 books and recorded thousands of messages.

THE EMBASSY OF GOD CHURCH

There are more than 300 rehabilitation centers for alcohol and drug addicts which have been operational in Ukraine and Europe since 1994.

More than 20,000 people recovered from their addictions, and became normal members of the society. Thanks to the rehabilitation centers opened by the church.

There are homes for abandoned street children operated by the church which have successfully reunited more than 5,000 children with their families.

The Embassy of God Church is involved in many social projects that are directed at maintaining family values, active civil involvement and individual fulfilment of church members.

Many former members of mafia organizations and criminals have become devout Christians through the missionary work of the Embassy of God Church.

The church's hot-line has counseled over a 200,000 people.

Right now there are over 25,000 members in the Embassy of God Church Kyiv, Ukraine.

BIOGRAPHY OF PASTOR SUNDAY ADELAJA

Pastor Sunday Adelaja is the Founder and Senior Pastor of The Embassy of the Blessed Kingdom of God for All Nations Church in Kyiv, Ukraine.

He is a Nigerian-born leader with an apostolic gift for the twenty-first century. In his mid thirties Pastor Sunday had already proven to be one of the world's most dynamic communicators and church planters and is regarded as the most successful pastor in Europe with over 25,000 members as well as daughter and satellite churches in over 50 countries worldwide.

The congregation includes members from all spheres of society, from former drug and alcohol addicts, to politicians and millionaires. It's high percentage of white Europeans (99%), also indicates that boundaries of racial prejudice have been surpassed. In the same country where Pastor Sunday was called "chocolate rabbit" and several attempts have been made to deport him, thousands join hands and support his mission to see Ukraine and the whole world affected and saved by the gospel of the Kingdom. Pastor Sunday is recognized as an unusually gifted teacher of the Word of God, with an extraordinary operation in the gifts of the Spirit, especially the word of knowledge. He receives numerous speaking invitations to several countries in all continents of the world yearly, as well as invitations to meetings with heads of States and other Politicians.

Pastor Sunday's influence in the areas of church growth, prayer and evangelism has been noted by Charisma Magazine, Ministries Today and many other Christian periodicals. The secular world media, such as the Wall Street Journal, Forbes, Washington Post, Reuters, Associated Press, CNN, BBC and German, Dutch and French national television have all widely reported on him. The Wall Street Journal called him "A Man with a Mission" set out to save Kyiv. The Ukrainian President Yushenko acknowledged his strong involvement in the Orange revolution for democracy in Ukraine. Former Mayor of New York City Rudolph Giuliani stated: *"Sunday, God bless you in your important mission. When I next come to Ukraine I would like to be at your church"*.

In August 2007 by invitation from the employees of the UN, Pastor Sunday Adelaja was invited as a speaker for three sessions. It was the first time in the history of the UN that a pastor speaks in the main hall of the UN. There were 500 organizations and missions from different parts of the world and leaders from 30 countries that participated in these sessions. From then on, the Embassy of God started its preparation to enter the UN and become a member of this organization.

Pastor Sunday's passion for National Transformation has driven him to maximally spread the word of God. He has written and published over 200 books of which some have been translated to English, German, Chinese, Arabic and Dutch. Also, thousands of sermons have been recorded. He organizes annual pastors leadership seminars where over 1,000 ministers regularly attend, studying the topic 'Pastoring without Tears'. His passion is to ignite these ministers with fire and power to transform their cities and countries.

Every year Pastor Sunday organizes Pastor's Seminars that take place in the church. He is also the main speaker there. During this time more than 1,000 Ministers learn how to be a pastor without tears, and learn the keys of achieving success. Also, every year Pastor Sunday organizes a summer and winter fast which aims at equipping Ministers with fire and power to change their cities and countries.

Nowadays, the apostolic ministry of Pastor Sunday has gone far beyond the boundaries of Ukraine, making him a desirable speaker and a Pastor to Pastors in many nations of the world. To date, he has visited over 50 countries.

Pastor Sunday is happily married to his "Princess" Abosede, and they are blessed with three children: Perez, Zoe and Pearl.

Below is the link to a photo gallery of Pastor Sunday and other likeminded individuals who have also positively impacted their nations:

http://www.godembassy.com/media/photo/view-album/3.html

FOLLOW SUNDAY ADELAJA
ON SOCIAL MEDIA

Subscribe And Read Pastor Sunday's Blog:

www.sundayadelajablog.com

Follow These Links And Listen To Over 200 Of Pastor Sunday`s Messages Free Of Charge:

http://sundayadelajablog.com/content/

Follow Pastor Sunday on Twitter:

www.twitter.com/official_pastor

Join Pastor Sunday's Facebook page to stay in touch:

www.facebook.com/pastor.sunday.adelaja

Visit our websites for more information about Pastor Sunday's ministry:

http://www.godembassy.com
http://www.pastorsunday.com
http://sundayadelaja.de

CONTACT

For distribution or to order bulk copies of this book, please contact us:

USA
CORNERSTONE PUBLISHING
info@thecornerstonepublishers.com
+1 (516) 547-4999
www.thecornerstonepublishers.com

AFRICA
Sunday Adelaja Media Ltd.
Email: btawolana@hotmail.com
+2348187518530, +2348097721451,
+2348034093699.

LONDON, UK
Pastor Abraham Great
abrahamagreat@gmail.com
+447711399828, +44-1908538141

KIEV, UKRAINE
pa@godembassy.org
Mobile: +380674401958

BEST SELLING BOOKS BY DR. SUNDAY ADELAJA

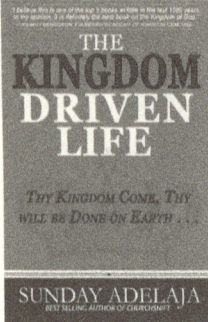

The Kingdom Driven Life:
Thy Kingdom Come, Thy Will be
Done on Earth
(Best seller)

Myles Munroe:
... Finding Answers To Why Good
People Die Tragic And Early Deaths

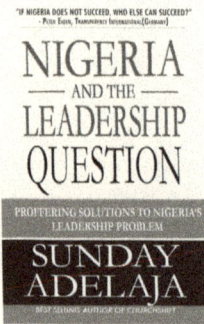

Nigeria And
The Leadership Question:
Proffering Solutions To Nigeria's
Leadership Problem

Olorunwa (There Is Sunday):
Portrait Of Sunday Adelaja.
The Roads Of Life.

AVAILABLE ON AMAZON AND OKADABOOKS.COM

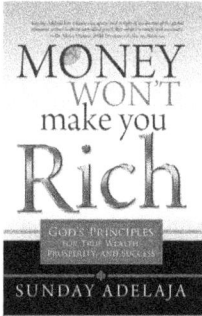

Money Won't Make You Rich:
God's Principles for True Wealth,
Prosperity, and Success

Who Am I? Why Am I here?:
How to discover your purpose and
calling in life

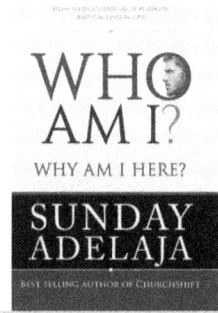

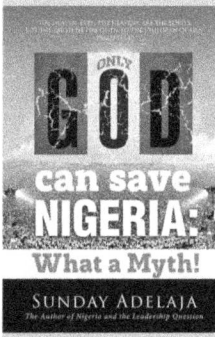

Only God Can Save Nigeria:
What a Myth?

Church Shift:
Revolutionizing Your Faith, Church,
and Life for the 21st Century

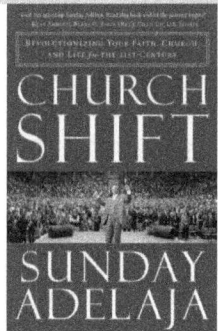

... and many more.

www.ingramcontent.com/pod-product-compliance
Lightning Source LLC
Chambersburg PA
CBHW022122080426
42734CB00006B/223